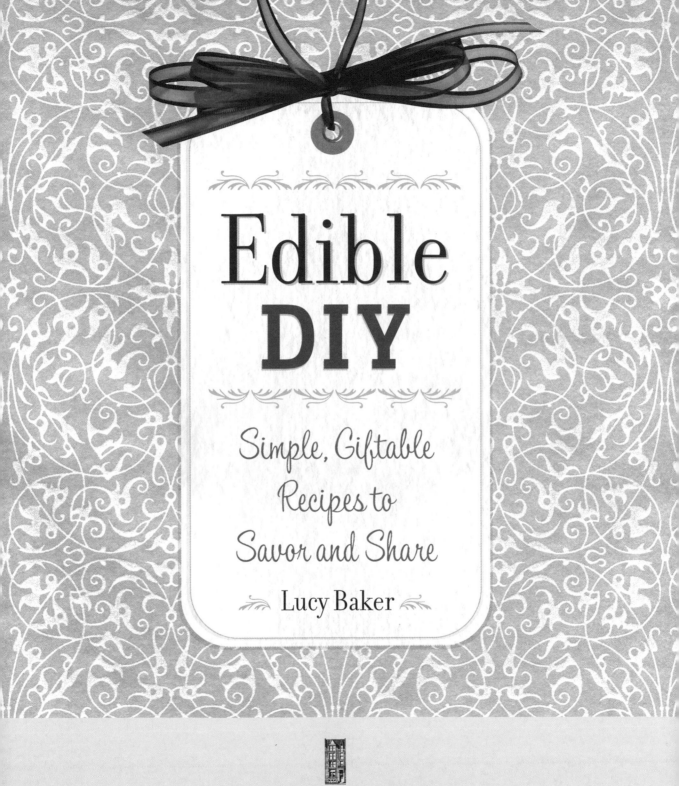

Edible DIY

Simple, Giftable Recipes to Savor and Share

Lucy Baker

RUNNING PRESS

PHILADELPHIA · LONDON

Books published by Running Press are available at special
discounts for bulk purchases in the United States by corpora-
tions, institutions, and other organizations. For more information,
please contact the Special Markets Department at the Perseus
Books Group, 2300 Chestnut Street, Suite 200, Philadelphia,
PA 19103, or call (800) 810-4145, ext. 5000, or e-mail special
.markets@perseusbooks.com.

ISBN 978-0-7624-4488-5
Library of Congress Control Number: 2012939654

E-book ISBN 978-0-7624-4688-9

9   8   7   6   5   4   3   2   1
Digit on the right indicates the number of this printing

Cover and interior book design and craft styling by Corinda Cook
Typography: Filosofia, Franklin Gothic, and Tamarillo
Edited by Geoffrey Stone

Photography by Steve Legato
Food Styling by Debbie Wahl
Photo Styling by Mariellen Melker
Special thanks to the following:
     Crate & Barrel, King of Prussia, PA
     Fante's, Philadelphia, PA
     Manor Home & Gifts, Philadelphia, PA
     Scarlett Alley, Philadelphia, PA

Running Press Book Publishers
A Member of the Perseus Books Group
2300 Chestnut Street
Philadelphia, PA 19103-4371

Visit us on the web!
www.runningpresscooks.com

Dedication

For my incredible and
amazing husband, Alex.
I love you.

Contents

Acknowledgments

First and foremost, thank you to my wonderful agent, Sharon Bowers, for her continued encouragement, support, and enthusiasm. A big thanks to Geoffrey Stone, my brilliant (and patient!) editor, and everyone else at Running Press: Seta Bedrossian Zink, Craig Herman, Corinda Cook, Steve Legato, Deborah Wahl, and Mariellen Melker.

As always, a huge thank-you to the entire team at Serious Eats, especially Erin Zimmer and Maggie Hoffman, for editing my weekly columns, and for agreeing with me that the best kind of gifts are those you can eat.

Thank you to my family: John and Elizabeth Baker, Jeffrey Baker, Susan and Larry Brandes, Jennifer, Chris, Beverly, and Shane Hepler. Lastly, thank you to my amazing husband, Alex, for all his love and support, and for cheerfully eating the good, the bad, and the burned.

Introduction

Four months after my now husband, Alex, and I started dating we took a trip to Portland, Oregon. On our last day we ate our way through the city's famed farmers' market, sampling crusty artisanal breads, gooey cheeses, homemade jams, and some of the juiciest blackberries I have ever tasted. Then we went to the Oregon Brewers Festival, where we sipped dozens of incredibly malty and hoppy microbrewed beers.

At the end of the day we collapsed, thoroughly stuffed, into our little rental car and drove to the airport. Alex was staying on the West Coast for another month, but I had to get back to New York for graduate school.

In the parking lot we hugged and kissed, and for the first time said, "I love you." Then I boarded the plane and flew home alone.

When you are newly in love, four weeks without your boyfriend can seem like an eternity. I wanted to call and e-mail Alex every day, but I also wanted to seem alluring and mysterious. I didn't want him to think I was desperate or clingy, and I wanted him to miss me, too. How could I show him how I felt about him without texting him every ten minutes?

I decided to make him pickles.

Sour dill pickles, to be precise. I set to work shopping for ingredients: crunchy miniature pickling cucumbers, fragrant fresh dill, pickling salt, vinegar, garlic, and black peppercorns and red pepper flakes for spice. I had never made pickles before, and I was surprised at how easy it turned out to be. Puttering around my sunny Brooklyn kitchen, I felt like a cross between Laura Ingalls Wilder and Nigella Lawson— a sort of quirky, prairie-style domestic goddess. When I was all finished, I packed my pickles into a pretty glass jar, taped on a label, and tied a piece of ribbon around the lid.

A few weeks later when Alex arrived home, I slid the jar of pickles into my purse and rode the bus over to his apartment. Standing on his doorstep I felt a great jumble of emotions: nervous, excited, scared, and impatient. We had been dating for less than six months, and he had been gone for a significant chunk of that time. What if he met someone else? What if he didn't say "I love you" again?

He opened the door. "I made you pickles," I blurted. And three years later, we got married.

If there is a better way to show your affection for someone than by making that person a delicious edible (or drinkable) gift, I'd like to know what it is. All my life I've been saying *thanks*, *I love you*, *I'm sorry*, or *I'm thinking of you* with food. I made Cornmeal Biscotti with Cranberries, Pecans, and White Chocolate (page 104) for the teachers who wrote me letters of recommendation, Chocolate-Covered Pretzel Toffee (page 92) for coworkers over the holidays, and—most famously in my family—twelve pounds of Spicy Pumpkin Seed–Pecan Brittle (page 37) to give out as favors at my own engagement party. (I got more compliments on the brittle than I did on my cute Anthropologie sundress, and people are still begging me for the recipe.) I've always abided by that old saying, "'tis better to give than to receive," but I'd add that best of all is to give something that you've made yourself.

People are always impressed when you present them with a homemade gift from your kitchen, be it a sack of Spicy Peanut Caramel Corn (page 38), a jar of Lavender Honey (page 101), or a jug of Strawberry-Watermelon Rum (page 59). "I can't believe you actually made this," or "you shouldn't have gone through the trouble," they invariably exclaim. But here is a secret: kitchen crafts are incredibly easy. Most of the recipes in this book can be prepared in less than an afternoon's time, and you don't have to be a culinary wunderkind for the results to look as delectably perfect as anything you would find on the shelf of your local gourmet food shop, or table at the farmers' market.

As a self-taught home cook, I understand exactly what makes some recipes totally doable and others intimidating. (I swear someday I'm going to try my hand at pulling taffy.) Nothing in this book requires fancy kitchen equipment or specialty ingredients that you must order over the Internet months in advance. In fact, I've made every effort to par the lists of ingredients down to the bare essentials. The point is to have fun and enjoy being creative in your kitchen, not to send you running to the store for Chinese five-spice powder or Himalayan rock salt. You don't have to be a *Top Chef*–worthy gourmand to prepare impressive, edible gifts that will delight your friends. In fact, it can be as easy as stuffing olives with blue cheese and almonds and packing them in a jar with some spices (Blue Cheese and Almond-Stuffed Olives, page 134), or whizzing cocoa and almonds in the food processor to form a paste to make Chocolate-Hazelnut Almond Spread (page 100).

I go to dinner parties a lot with my friends, and we invariably ask each other, "What can I bring?" More often than not we show up with a six-pack of beer, a bottle of wine off the $10 table, or a wedge of cheap-but-decent domestic Brie. How much more fun would it be to present your host with a container of Sweet and Spicy Walnuts (page 33) to set out alongside the appetizers, a box of Raspberry–Goat Cheese Truffles (page 93) to go with dessert, or a jar of peak-of-the-season Peach Jam with Lavender and Honey (page 158) she can enjoy the next day with breakfast?

Making your own food gifts isn't only easy, it's economical, too. You can whip up eight jars of jam for about the same amount of money you would spend on two jars at the farmers' market. Bottom-shelf gin is transformed into a fancy aperitif when infused with juicy pears and heady spices (Spiced Pear Gin, page 64). And spicy Chili-Lime Peanuts (page 35) can be made for . . . well, peanuts. In addition, most of these recipes can be divided into multiple gifts, making them perfect for party favors and holidays. Bake one batch of Cornmeal Biscotti with Cranberries, Pecans, and White Chocolate (page 104), and you can knock four people off your list. You don't have to shell out big bucks to show the people in your life that you care. Saying I love you can be as simple—and impressive—as offering them a bottle of homemade ketchup (Chipotle Ketchup, page 122).

I'm confident that you will find something to make for everyone you know within these pages. There are salty and crunchy snacks, sweet candies and desserts, spicy pickles and condiments, and fruity jams and conserves. I've also included an entire chapter of homemade boozy gifts—but don't worry, you don't need to set up a distillery in your basement or spend a fortune on home-brewing equipment. These are simple infusions anyone can prepare in minutes, and you can leave them to infuse in the back of your closet behind your shoes. All the recipes have a shelf life of at least a week (and usually several months), so you can make them in advance, or ship them to a friend on the opposite coast.

What are you waiting for? So what if you've only ever made toast? Soon, you'll be slathering it with your very own homemade Pistachio-Honey Butter (page 102), Vanilla-Orange Marmalade (page 152), or Concord Grape Jam (page 162).

A Year of Edible Gifts

With the exception of some of the jams and liqueurs that use seasonal fruits, the recipes in this book can be prepared at any point during the year. But just because you can make Chocolate Barbecue Sauce (page 126) in February doesn't mean you should. Here are some suggestions for what to make and give throughout the year.

New Year's Day

Start the New Year off with a little something healthy!

Triple Coconut Granola (page 47)

Pecan Granola Bars (page 48)

Winter Fig Jam (page 167)

Dill-Pickled Brussel Sprouts (page 138)

Super Bowl Party

Man-friendly treats easy to snack on without tearing your eyes from the television.

Chili-Lime Peanuts (page 35)

Curried Cashews (page 30)

Apple-Cinnamon Bourbon (page 66)

Chocolate-Covered Pretzel Toffee (page 92)

Cinnamon-Raisin Buckeyes (page 83)

Compost Bark (page 82)

Pineapple Salsa (page 131)

Root Beer Jerky (page 137)

Valentine's Day

Skip the clichéd dozen roses and box of chocolates and surprise your sweetie
with something homemade, delicious, and incredibly romantic.

Crema di Limoncello (page 72)

Chocolate-Hazelnut Almond Spread (page 100)

Raspberry-Lime Liqueur (page 61)

Whiskey Butterscotch Sauce (page 98)

Dark Chocolate-Dipped Orangettes (page 95)

Raspberry–Goat Cheese Truffles (page 93)

Maple Syrup Caramels with Fleur de Sel (page 88)

Oscar Party

Easy and elegant party snacks. Don't forget the Champagne!

Herbs de Provence Popcorn (page 46)

Thai-Spiced Potato Chips (page 41)

Everything Breadsticks (page 44)

Sweet and Spicy Walnuts (page 33)

Curried Cashews (page 30)

Passover/Easter

Gifts to celebrate spring.

Spicy Marinated Artichoke Hearts (page 132)

Pistachio-Honey Butter (page 102)

Carrot Cake Conserve (page 150)

Lavender Honey (page 101)

Mother's Day

Perfect gifts for moms, mothers-in-law, and grandmas.

Flavored Salts (page 114–119)

Vanilla-Orange Marmalade (page 152)

Vin d'Orange (page 71)

Pickled Fennel (page 136)

Lavender Honey (page 101)

Strawberry-Balsamic-Thyme Jam (page 157)

Strawberry Rosé *Pâte de Fruits* (page 96)

Blueberry-Port Jam (page 155)

Father's Day

From boozy cherries to dress up his drink, to condiments that add kick to his backyard grill fests, these are gifts Dad will love.

Brandied Cherries **(page 97)**

Chocolate-Covered Pretzel Toffee **(page 92)**

Balsamic-Raisin Steak Sauce **(page 127)**

Honey-Beer Mustard **(page 125)**

Chipotle Ketchup **(page 122)**

Bacon-Chocolate Biscotti **(page 103)**

Bread-and-Butter Zucchini Relish **(page 133)**

Fourth of July/Labor Day Barbecue

Skip the six-pack and bring one of these treats to your next summer pool party!

Barbecue Potato Chips **(page 40)**

Strawberry-Watermelon Rum **(page 59)**

Pineapple-Mango Tequila **(page 58)**

Lemony Sweet Tea Vodka **(page 56)**

Chocolate Barbecue Sauce **(page 126)**

Chipotle Ketchup **(page 122)**

Rosh Hashanah

Sweet apple and honey gifts to celebrate the Jewish New Year.

Lavender Honey **(page 101)**

Slow Cooker Caramel Apple Butter **(page 147)**

Apple Cider Jelly **(page 146)**

Pistachio-Honey Butter **(page 102)**

Halloween

Candy, pumpkin, and apples galore! These fall-friendly gifts will appeal to the kid in everyone!

Honey-Ginger Pumpkin Butter **(page 151)**

Compost Bark **(page 82)**

Maple Syrup Caramels with Fleur de Sel **(page 88)**

Chocolate-Covered Pretzel Toffee **(page 92)**

Apple-Cinnamon Bourbon **(page 66)**

Spicy Pumpkin Seed–Pecan Brittle **(page 37)**

Spicy Peanut Caramel Corn **(page 38)**

Thanksgiving

Condiments perfect for dressing up leftovers, perfect predinner snacks,
and bourbon to soothe frazzled nerves.

My Nana's Buttered Almonds (page 34)

Apple-Cinnamon Bourbon (page 66)

Fig and Onion Marmalade (page 168)

Apple Cider Jelly (page 146)

Dill-Pickled Brussels Sprouts (page 138)

Christmas

Decadent treats to sip and savor in front of a roaring fire, or stuff inside a stocking.

Spiced Pear Gin **(page 64)**

Minty Irish Cream Liqueur **(page 69)**

White Chocolate Fudge with Bourbon and Pecans

   (page 79)

Gingersnap Balls **(page 85)**

Winter Fig Jam **(page 167)**

Cornmeal Biscotti with Cranberries, Pecans, and White

   Chocolate **(page 104)**

Cranberry-Champagne Jam with Crystallized Ginger

   (page 164)

Kid's Party

Sweets that make perfect kid-friendly party favors.

Pecan Granola Bars **(page 48)**

Peppermint Marshmallows **(page 86)**

Compost Bark **(page 82)**

Cinnamon-Raisin Buckeyes **(page 83)**

Maple Walnut Graham Crackers **(page 106)**

Chocolate-Hazelnut Almond Spread **(page 100)**

Hostess

Simple, inspired gifts to take to your next dinner party.

Blue Cheese and Almond-Stuffed Olives **(page 134)**

Cacio e Pepe Crackers **(page 43)**

Cucumber-Jalapeño Vodka **(page 63)**

Raspberry–Goat Cheese Truffles **(page 93)**

Crunchy

Curried Cashews

Sweet and Spicy Walnuts

My Nana's Buttered Almonds

Chili-Lime Peanuts

Spicy Pumpkin Seed—Pecan Brittle

Spicy Peanut Caramel Corn

Barbecue Potato Chips

Thai-Spiced Potato Chips

Cacio e Pepe Crackers

Everything Breadsticks

Herbs de Provence Popcorn

Triple Coconut Granola

Pecan Granola Bars

A few years ago, I made a big batch of spiced nuts to take along to a friend's Halloween party. When they were finished, I took them out of the oven and set them on the windowsill to cool, allowing their buttery, toasty aroma to fill the air. A few minutes later I turned around to find a squirrel inside my kitchen! He was sitting on top of the radiator beneath the window, up on his haunches, nose pointed toward the baking sheet, whiskers quivering. I let out a yelp and, fortunately, he scampered back onto the fire escape before he could steal a single almond. And really, I couldn't blame him. He knew what was up. Salty, crunchy, homemade spiced nuts are intoxicating and irresistible. Obviously, he just couldn't help himself.

What is it about crispy, crackly snacks that make them so addictive? I find it literally impossible to keep my hands out of a bowl of Chili-Lime Peanuts (page 35), and I've snuck a bag of Herbs de Provence Popcorn (page 46) into the movie theater on more than one occasion. The recipes in this chapter are perfect for munching, from my grandmother's time-tested rendition of butter-roasted almonds, My Nana's Buttered Almonds (page 34), to Thai-Spiced Potato Chips (page 41). I've also included a few recipes that incorporate a bit of sugar in with the crunch, like Sweet and Spicy Walnuts (page 33) and Triple Coconut Granola (page 47).

In addition to being great snacks, these recipes also make ideal hostess gifts. I know when I'm throwing a dinner party I plan the menu out weeks in advance, from the cocktails to the dessert. I wouldn't want someone to show up with a salad or a pie that didn't fit with my meal, or worse, stole the show. But a small, unassuming-yet-impressive token, such as a box of *Cacio e Pepe* Crackers (page 43) or tin of Spicy Pumpkin Seed–Pecan Brittle (page 37) is perfect.

Many of these recipes are also easy to multiply. All of the nuts, the granola, and the Spicy Peanut Caramel Corn (page 38) can be prepared in big batches and then divided up to make party favors. When my husband and I got married, I made loads of Curried Cashews (page 30), and we left bags of them in the hotel rooms of all our guests along with a bottle of our favorite local beer. It was an easy, inexpensive, and personal way to say thanks to our friends and family.

Curried Cashews

These cashews are an irresistible combination of spicy, salty, and sweet. If you're concerned about the heat level, dial the curry back to two teaspoons and the cayenne back to a quarter teaspoon. Don't wrinkle your nose at the egg whites. They might seem like an odd ingredient, but they bind the spices to the nuts without adding extra grease. The results are nuts that stay toasted and crunchy for up to a month.

MAKES 3 CUPS

3 cups raw, unsalted cashews

2 tablespoons packed dark
   brown sugar

1 tablespoon kosher salt

1 tablespoon curry powder

½ teaspoon ground cumin

½ teaspoon cayenne

2 large egg whites

Adjust a rack in the center of the oven and preheat the oven to 400°F. Spread the cashews in a single layer on a parchment-lined baking sheet and bake them until they are just beginning to turn golden, about 7 minutes. Remove from the oven and let the nuts cool completely, about 30 minutes. Leave the oven on.

Meanwhile, combine the brown sugar, salt, curry powder, cumin, and cayenne in a medium bowl.

Once the nuts have cooled, beat the egg whites in a medium bowl with an electric mixer until they are very frothy, about 2 minutes. Add the cashews and toss to coat evenly. Strain the cashews through a fine mesh sieve to remove the excess egg whites.

Transfer the cashews to the bowl with the spices and toss well to coat. Spread the cashews back onto the baking sheet and bake for 5 minutes. Stir the cashews and bake until the cashews are fragrant and golden brown, another 4 to 5 minutes.

Sweet and Spicy Walnuts

Once, when I was pressed for time and hosting a dinner party, I picked up a container of spiced walnuts at Whole Foods instead of making them myself. Much to my dismay, everyone raved about them and begged for the recipe! After carefully studying the ingredient list, I came up with this interpretation. What I like best about these nuts is the thick, crusty layer of salt, spice, and sugar on the surface. I like to serve them with olives and *Cacio e Pepe* Crackers (page 43) before dinner. They will keep for about a month, stored in an airtight container at room temperature.

MAKES 4 CUPS

4 cups whole walnut halves

$^2/_3$ cup sugar

2 teaspoons kosher salt

1 $^1/_2$ teaspoons chipotle chili powder

1 teaspoon cinnamon

$^1/_2$ teaspoon cayenne

Pinch of ground cloves (optional)

1 large egg white

Adjust a rack in the center of the oven and preheat the oven to 350°F. Spread the walnuts in a single layer on a parchment-lined baking sheet and bake until they are toasted and fragrant, about 7 minutes. Remove from the oven and let the nuts cool completely, about 30 minutes. Leave the oven on.

Meanwhile, in a medium bowl, combine the sugar, salt, chili powder, cinnamon, cayenne, and cloves.

Once the nuts have cooled, beat the egg white in a medium bowl with an electric mixer until it is very frothy, about 2 minutes. Add the walnuts and toss to coat evenly. If necessary, strain the walnuts through a fine mesh sieve to remove the excess egg whites.

Transfer the walnuts to the bowl with the sugar mixture and toss well to coat. Spread the walnuts back onto the baking sheet and bake for 5 minutes. Stir the nuts and bake until they are fragrant and golden brown, 5 to 10 minutes.

My Nana's Buttered Almonds

My nana wasn't exactly known for her sophisticated palate or culinary talents. Her favorite breakfast was a wedge of cantaloupe sprinkled liberally with salt and pepper (who else, I ask you, salts their melons?), and she once fed me a raw hot dog for lunch. But every year at Christmas, she turned out the most delicious, crunchy, salty, buttery almonds. How could three basic ingredients yield such amazing results? There are two simple tricks. The first is to drain the buttered almonds immediately after they come out of the oven. This ensures that they crisp up nicely. The second is to double salt them—first before they are roasted and then again as they are cooling. These almonds pair especially well with rich, creamy cheeses like Brie.

MAKES 3 CUPS

3 cups blanched almonds

2 tablespoons unsalted butter, melted

2 teaspoons or more fleur de sel, or kosher salt

Preheat the oven to 350°F and line a baking sheet with parchment paper. Toss the almonds and butter together in a large bowl. Spread the almonds on the baking sheet and sprinkle with half the salt. Bake the almonds, stirring occasionally, until they are fragrant and golden brown, about 20 minutes.

Meanwhile, line another baking sheet with paper towels. When the almonds are toasted, scrape them onto the paper towel–lined baking sheet to drain. Taste one and sprinkle with more salt as necessary. When the almonds have cooled completely, about 30 minutes, transfer them to an airtight container and store at room temperature for up to 1 month.

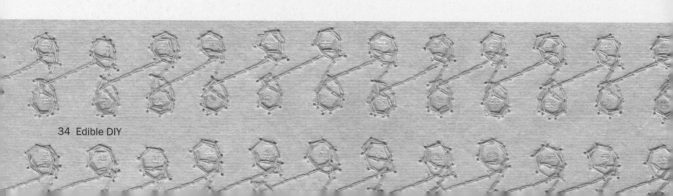

Chili-Lime Peanuts

The humble peanut is often overlooked for the fancier pecan or almond. I think that's a shame! One of the best things about peanuts is that they are wallet-friendly. This entire recipe can be made for less than five dollars. Chili-Lime Peanuts are completely addictive and absolutely perfect for munching with a cold beer or, better yet, a margarita. The zingy lime flavor is a cool complement to the spicy chili powder and cayenne. A pinch of sugar balances out the salt and heat. They will keep for about one month, stored in an airtight container at room temperature.

MAKES 4 CUPS

$1/4$ cup freshly squeezed lime juice (2 or 3 large limes)

2 teaspoons freshly grated lime zest (1 small lime)

2 tablespoons chili powder

1 tablespoon kosher salt

2 teaspoons sugar

$3/4$ teaspoon cayenne

4 cups shelled unsalted peanuts

Preheat the oven to 250°F. Whisk lime juice, lime zest, chili powder, salt, sugar, and cayenne pepper together in a large bowl. Add peanuts and stir until evenly coated. Scrape nuts onto a large, rimmed baking sheet. Bake until the nuts are fragrant, dry, and beginning to darken, about 30 minutes.

Spicy Pumpkin Seed— Pecan Brittle

I made a version of this nut brittle to give out as favors at my own engagement party. It was a total hit—I got more compliments on the brittle than I did on my dress! It's a snap to make (pun intended), and the flavors are pure fall: crackly pumpkin seeds, crunchy pecans, and warm cinnamon. The cayenne adds the subtlest hint of heat, and the fleur de sel makes it dangerously addictive. For more of a kick, increase the cayenne to $^1/_2$ teaspoon. Or for a pie-inspired version, omit the cayenne and cinnamon and add $^3/_4$ teaspoon of pumpkin pie spice along with the baking soda.

MAKES ABOUT 1½ POUNDS

2 cups sugar

$^1/_2$ cup water

$^1/_4$ pound (1 stick) unsalted butter, diced

$^1/_4$ cup light corn syrup

$^1/_2$ teaspoon cinnamon

$^1/_4$ teaspoon cayenne

$^1/_2$ teaspoon baking soda

6 ounces toasted pumpkin seeds (about 1$^3/_4$ cups)

6 ounces toasted pecans (about 1$^1/_2$ cups)

1$^1/_2$ teaspoons flaky salt, such as fleur de sel

Line a baking sheet with parchment paper. Set aside.

Combine the sugar, water, butter, and corn syrup in a medium-sized pot and bring it to a boil over medium-high heat. Cook, stirring occasionally, until the mixture is a rich amber color and a candy thermometer registers 300°F. Be patient, this can take up to 20 minutes.

When the thermometer hits 300°F, immediately remove the pot from the heat and stir in the cinnamon, cayenne, and baking soda. The mixture will bubble and foam vigorously. Stir in the pumpkin seeds and the pecans. Immediately scrape the brittle onto the parchment-lined baking sheet, spreading it out as much as possible with the back of a spoon. Sprinkle the salt over the hot brittle. Using clean fingertips, gently press as many of the salt crystals as you can into the brittle. This helps them to stick once the brittle is firm.

Allow the brittle to cool completely, about 2 hours, then break it into large shards. The brittle will keep for up to 3 weeks stored in an airtight container at room temperature.

Spicy Peanut Caramel Corn

When I was in college, my roommates and I had an ancient air popper that we used almost every night to make massive batches of poststudy session popcorn. We got pretty crazy with flavorings—our favorite involved a whole lot of hot sauce. This Spicy Peanut Caramel Corn always makes me wistful for my dorm room days. Think of it as Cracker Jacks for grown-ups. I love the peanuts in this recipe because they remind me of baseball games, but you could use pecans for a more sophisticated version. Watch the caramel corn carefully when it is in the oven and make sure to get to the corners when you stir so that it doesn't burn.

MAKES ABOUT 12 CUPS

2 tablespoons canola or vegetable oil

1/2 cup popcorn kernels

2 1/2 cups roasted, salted peanuts

1/4 pound (1 stick) unsalted butter

1 cup packed dark brown sugar

1/2 cup light corn syrup

1 teaspoon coarse kosher salt

1/4 teaspoon baking soda

1/2 teaspoon pure vanilla extract

1/2 teaspoon chili powder

1/4 teaspoon cayenne

First make the popcorn. Pour the oil into a large, deep heavy-bottomed pot with a tight-fitting lid and heat over medium-high heat until hot but not smoking. Drop 3 or 4 popcorn kernels into the pot and cover. When you hear them pop, the oil is ready. Add the remaining kernels and cover. Cook, shaking the pot back and forth over the burner, holding down the lid, until the popping slows almost to a stop, about 3 or 4 minutes.

Transfer the popcorn to a large bowl and add the peanuts. Preheat the oven to 200°F. Line a baking sheet with parchment paper.

In a medium saucepan, combine the butter, brown sugar, corn syrup, and salt. Bring it to a boil over medium heat. Reduce heat to medium-low, clip a candy thermometer to the side of the pan, and continue to cook, stirring occasionally, until the mixture reaches 238°F. Immediately remove the pan from the heat and stir in the baking soda, vanilla, chili powder, and cayenne.

Pour the hot caramel over the popcorn and peanuts and toss until evenly coated. Transfer the popcorn mixture to a baking sheet and bake for 40 minutes, stirring once halfway through. The caramel corn will keep for 2 to 3 weeks, stored in an airtight container at room temperature.

Barbecue Potato Chips

I can honestly say I never met a potato chip I didn't like, but barbecue might be my favorite. You might be surprised to learn that you probably already have all the spices you need to create an authentic barbecue flavor in your pantry: brown sugar, garlic powder, chili powder, and paprika. These chips aren't difficult to make, but be sure to leave yourself plenty of time to soak and dry the potato slices. Bring a batch to your next cookout or pool party.

MAKES ABOUT 10 CUPS,
ENOUGH TO SERVE ALONG-
SIDE 4 TO 6 SANDWICHES

2 large russet potatoes

1 tablespoon packed dark
    brown sugar

1 tablespoon kosher salt

1/2 teaspoon garlic powder

1/2 teaspoon chili powder

1/2 teaspoon paprika

Peanut or vegetable oil for frying

Fill a large bowl with cold water. Cut the potatoes in half crosswise. Using a mandoline, thinly slice each half into rounds. Transfer the potato slices to the water and let them soak for 1 hour. Meanwhile, combine the brown sugar, salt, garlic powder, chili powder, and paprika in a small bowl. Line a work surface with a layer of newspaper and then a layer of paper towels.

Drain the potatoes and lay them in a single layer on top of the paper towels. Let them stand until dry, about 30 minutes. Blot any damp spots with extra paper towels.

Pour 2 or 3 inches of oil in a large pot, such as a Dutch oven. Clip a thermometer to the side of the pot and heat over medium-high heat until the oil reaches 375°F. While the oil is heating, transfer the potato slices to a clean, dry bowl and reline the work surface with a new layer of newspaper and paper towels. Line a large, flat plate with paper towels. Have ready a clean paper shopping bag.

Working in batches, fry the potato slices, turning once, until they are nicely browned, 2 to 4 minutes. Remove the chips as they are done with a slotted spoon and transfer them to the paper towel–lined plate. From the plate, dump the chips into the paper bag and sprinkle with a little bit of the spice mixture. Give the bag a good shake to coat the chips. Dump the chips out onto the work surface lined with newspaper and paper towels and let them drain and dry completely.

Store the chips in an airtight container for up to a month.

Thai-Spiced Potato Chips

These days you can find potato chips in all sorts of wacky flavors. This recipe is my version of the delicious Spicy Thai Potato Chips made by Kettle Chips. It combines the classic Thai flavors (salty, sour, spicy, and sweet) with a whole lot of crunch. These chips are absolutely delicious with an ice-cold beer on a hot summer day.

MAKES ABOUT 10 CUPS, ENOUGH TO SERVE ALONGSIDE 4 TO 6 SANDWICHES

2 large russet potatoes

2 tablespoons freshly grated
   lime zest (3 medium limes)

1 tablespoon packed dark
   brown sugar

1 tablespoon kosher salt

1/2 teaspoon garlic powder

1/4 teaspoon ground ginger

1/2 teaspoon ground Thai chiles,
   or chili powder

Peanut or vegetable oil for frying

Fill a large bowl with cold water. Cut the potatoes in half crosswise. Using a mandoline, thinly slice each half into rounds. Transfer the potato slices to the water and let them soak for 1 hour. Meanwhile, combine the lime zest, brown sugar, salt, garlic powder, ground ginger, and chili powder in a small bowl. Line a work surface with a layer of newspaper and then a layer of paper towels.

Drain the potatoes and lay them in a single layer on top of the paper towels. Let them stand until dry, about 30 minutes. Blot any damp spots with extra paper towels.

Pour 2 or 3 inches of oil in a large pot, such as a Dutch oven. Clip a thermometer to the side of the pot and heat over medium-high heat until the oil reaches 375°F. While the oil is heating, transfer the potato slices to a clean, dry bowl and reline the work surface with a new layer of newspaper and paper towels. Line a large, flat plate with paper towels. Have ready a clean paper shopping bag.

Working in batches, fry the potato slices, turning once, until they are nicely browned, 2 to 4 minutes. Remove the chips as they are done with a slotted spoon and transfer them to the paper towel–lined plate. From the plate, dump the chips into the paper bag and sprinkle with a little bit of the spice mixture. Give the bag a good shake to coat the chips. Dump the chips out onto the work surface lined with newspaper and paper towels and let them drain and dry completely.

Store the chips in an airtight container for up to 1 month.

Cacio e Pepe Crackers

One of my favorite places to eat in New York City is Lupa, an Italian restaurant in the West Village. I can never resist the *bavette cacio e pepe*, a stunningly simple pasta dish adorned with nothing more than pecorino cheese and black pepper. I've incorporated those flavors into these slice-and-bake crackers. They make a wonderful, fuss-free hors d'oeuvre and are just the thing with a glass of chilled Prosecco. You can make the dough up to a week in advance and bake the crackers up to three days in advance. This recipe is based upon one you will often see with blue cheese, which not everyone loves (Ina Garten makes a wonderful version with walnuts). I like pecorino because it has loads of flavor but isn't quite as funky.

MAKES ABOUT 30 CRACKERS

1 $^1/_2$ cups all-purpose flour

$^1/_2$ teaspoon kosher salt

2 teaspoons freshly ground
   black pepper

1 cup grated Pecorino Romano
   cheese

8 tablespoons (1 stick) cold
   unsalted butter, diced

Combine the flour, salt, and pepper in the bowl of a food processor and pulse to combine. Add the cheese and pulse to incorporate. Add the butter and pulse until the mixture is coarsely combined and looks like wet sand. Slowly drizzle in 1 to 2 tablespoons of cold water, and pulse until the mixture begins to come together in a ball.

Turn the dough out onto a lightly floured work surface and shape it into a 12-inch log. Wrap the log in plastic and refrigerate for at least 1 hour and up to 1 week.

Position an oven rack in the middle of the oven and preheat the oven to 350°F. Line a baking sheet with parchment paper. Cut the log of dough crosswise into $^1/_4$- to $^1/_2$-inch-thick rounds. Transfer to the baking sheet and bake until the crackers are very lightly browned, 20 to 25 minutes.

Store the crackers in an airtight container for up to 2 weeks.

Everything Breadsticks

On Sunday mornings, the bagel shop around the corner from my apartment in Brooklyn sells out of everything bagels fast. They are everyone's favorite, for obvious reasons: the nutty crunch of sesame and poppy seeds, the fragrant garlic, and the generous sprinkling of coarse salt. Store-bought puff pastry makes these breadsticks a breeze. They make an elegant hors d'oeuvre on their own or wrapped with a thin slice of smoked salmon. With a breadstick in one hand and a bellini or mimosa in the other, you're sure to be a happy camper.

MAKES 26 TO 28 BREADSTICKS

2 tablespoons sesame seeds

2 tablespoons poppy seeds

2 teaspoons granulated garlic

2 teaspoons kosher salt

¼ teaspoon onion powder

1 (17.3-ounce) package frozen puff pastry sheets, such as Pepperidge Farm, defrosted

All-purpose flour for dusting

4 tablespoons (½ stick) unsalted butter, melted

Preheat the oven to 375°F. Line a baking sheet with parchment paper.

In a small bowl, combine the sesame seeds, poppy seeds, granulated garlic, salt, and onion powder.

Unfold the puff pastry sheets on a lightly floured work surface. Roll them out gently with a rolling pin, just to smooth out the creases. Cut each strip lengthwise into 13 or 14 thin strips. Brush each strip with melted butter and sprinkle with the sesame seed mixture. Twist each strip several times to create a "tendril" effect.

Place the strips on the baking sheet and bake until they are puffed and golden brown, 12 to 15 minutes. Cool the breadsticks completely on a wire rack, about 30 minutes.

Store the breadsticks in an airtight container for up to 5 days.

Herbs de Provence Popcorn

This French-inspired popcorn is seasoned with herbs de Provence, a blend of herbs commonly found in the south of France including savory, rosemary, thyme, fennel, marjoram, and lavender. Don't worry; you don't have to buy them all! You can purchase jars of premixed herbs de Provence at most grocery stores. This popcorn makes an elegant, fuss-free Oscar party snack. It's the most delicious the day it's made, but it will keep well for up to three days in an airtight container. Pack small portions into cellophane bags and tie them with ribbon to make pretty (and cheap!) party favors.

MAKES ABOUT 12 CUPS

$^1/_2$ cup extra-virgin olive oil

2 $^1/_2$ teaspoons herbs de Provence, divided

1 garlic clove, peeled and smashed

$^3/_4$ cup popcorn kernels

Kosher salt to taste

Combine the olive oil, 2 teaspoons of the herbs de Provence, and garlic in a small saucepan. Cook over medium-low heat until the oil is fragrant, about 5 minutes. Remove the pan from the heat and allow the oil to cool completely. Strain the oil through a fine mesh sieve into a small bowl. Discard the herbs and garlic.

Heat 4 tablespoons of the infused oil in a large, deep heavy-bottomed pot with a tight fitting lid and heat over medium-high heat until hot but not smoking. Drop 3 or 4 popcorn kernels into the pot and cover. When you hear them pop, the oil is ready. Add the remaining kernels and cover. Cook, shaking the pot back and forth over the burner, holding down the lid, until the popping slows almost to a stop, about 3 or 4 minutes.

Transfer the popcorn to a large bowl and drizzle with the remaining infused oil. Sprinkle with $^1/_2$ teaspoon herbs de Provence and kosher salt to taste.

Triple Coconut Granola

What could be better than coconut granola? How about triple coconut granola? You can find shredded unsweetened coconut and virgin coconut oil at almost any health-food store. Be sure to use virgin coconut oil, which packs much more flavor than regular coconut oil. If you can't find it, vegetable oil is a fine substitute—but you'll have to call it double coconut granola. If you're not a raisin fan, you can substitute any other dried fruit.

MAKES ABOUT 8 CUPS

3 cups rolled oats

1 $^1/_2$ cups slivered almonds,
   roughly chopped

1 cup shredded unsweetened
   coconut

1 cup shredded sweetened
   coconut

$^1/_3$ cup packed dark brown
   sugar

$^1/_2$ teaspoon cinnamon

$^1/_4$ teaspoon kosher salt

$^1/_2$ cup virgin coconut oil

2 tablespoons honey or maple
   syrup

1 $^1/_2$ cups golden raisins

Preheat the oven to 325°F.

Combine the oats, slivered almonds, unsweetened coconut, sweetened coconut, brown sugar, cinnamon, and salt in a large bowl. Add the coconut oil and honey and stir until all the ingredients are well combined.

Spread the mixture on a large rimmed baking sheet and bake, stirring occasionally, until the granola is golden brown, 25 to 30 minutes. (If the oats seem to be darkening too quickly, turn the temperature down to 300°F.)

Remove the granola from the oven and allow it to cool completely on the baking sheet, about 45 minutes. Stir in the raisins. The granola will keep well for 2 or 3 weeks, stored in an airtight container at room temperature.

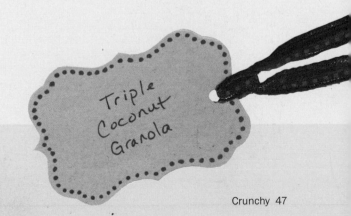

Triple
Coconut
Granola

Pecan Granola Bars

These moist, chewy granola bars remind me of the Quaker Oats granola bars I used to gobble as a kid after field hockey practice. In this recipe I use whole wheat flour to make them a bit healthier, but if you don't have any on hand, all-purpose will do just fine. Feel free to play around with the dried fruit and nuts—use dried strawberries and peanuts, dried cherries and almonds, or dried figs and walnuts. Pack the bars in a pretty box or tin and give them to your most outdoorsy friend.

Makes 24 Bars

2 cups rolled oats

1 cup shredded unsweetened coconut

1 cup pecans, chopped

1 ¹/₂ cup raisins

¹/₂ cup dried apricots, chopped

1 cup whole wheat flour or all-purpose flour

³/₄ teaspoon cinnamon

¹/₂ teaspoon baking powder

¹/₄ teaspoon salt

¹/₄ pound (1 stick) unsalted butter, softened

³/₄ cup packed brown sugar

¹/₄ cup honey

1 large egg

1 teaspoon vanilla extract

Position a rack in the center of the oven and preheat the oven to 350°F. Spray a 13 x 9-inch baking pan with nonstick spray and line the bottom with parchment paper.

In a medium bowl, stir together the oats, coconut, pecans, raisins and dried apricots. In a separate small bowl, stir together the flour, cinnamon, baking powder, and salt.

In a large bowl, combine the butter, brown sugar, and honey. Beat with an electric mixer until light and fluffy, about 2 minutes. Add the egg and the vanilla extract, and beat until incorporated.

Gradually beat the flour mixture into the butter mixture just until combined. Stir in the oat mixture with a wooden spoon.

Press the mixture evenly into the prepared pan. Bake until the top is golden and the edges are lightly brown, about 25 minutes. The bars will be very soft straight from the oven, but will firm up as they cool. Cool them completely on a wire rack, then cut into bars. They will keep for up to 10 days stored in an airtight container at room temperature.

Boozy

Lemony Sweet Tea Vodka

Pineapple-Mango Tequila

Strawberry-Watermelon Rum

Raspberry-Lime Liqueur

Peachy Bourbon (Homemade Southern Comfort)

Cucumber-Jalapeño Vodka

Spiced Pear Gin

Apple-Cinnamon Bourbon

Minty Irish Cream Liqueur

Ginger Liqueur

Vin d'Orange

Crema di Limoncello

Recently, a few of my friends have gotten into making homemade beer. The process is fascinating and the results are delicious, but the equipment is expensive and bulky. One friend has turned his whole laundry room into a virtual brewery, with fermenting buckets on top of the washer and dryer, and plastic tubes snaking every which way. Every time I'm there I half expect Bill Nye the Science Guy to pop up from behind a giant keg.

While I'm impressed with my friends' ambition (and while I love to drink the fruits of their labor!), I'm not going to turn into a brewmaster myself any time soon. I just don't have the time, the space, or the funds for all that crazy beer gear. Besides, I've found that it is possible to create sumptuous and impressive infused alcohols with minimal time and effort, and no special equipment—in fact, I can make them in the back of my closet behind my shoes.

The recipes in this chapter are for simple, elegant alcohols infused with juicy fruits, heady spices, and maybe even a little something chocolaty. Once prepared, most of the liqueurs last for months or even years, so you can sip last summer's Raspberry-Lime

Raspberry
Lime Liqu...

Liqueur (page 61) in front of next winter's fire, or use your bottle of homemade Cucumber-Jalapeño Vodka (page 63) to make Bloody Marys at every Sunday brunch. Minty Irish Cream Liqueur (page 69), Spiced Pear Gin (page 64), and Ginger Liqueur (page 70) are obvious choices for holiday gifts, but I would also encourage you to be creative and plan ahead. Why not make a big batch of Strawberry-Watermelon Rum (page 59) in August and stash it away until December? A little taste of the tropics would be a welcome addition to any Christmas stocking.

A note about ingredients: since they provide most of the flavor, it is imperative to use peak-of-the season fruits and fresh spices in these recipes. However, the alcohol doesn't need to be anything special. Save your small batch bourbons and fancy vodkas! Mid- to bottom-shelf varieties will do just fine. When testing these recipes, I used liquors in the fifteen- to twenty-dollar-per-liter range. While they are simple to prepare, some of these liqueurs require a degree of patience. It can take a few weeks for the alcohol to mellow, sweeten, and fully take on the flavor of the fruit. That said, don't be tempted to let them sit any longer than directed, either, as they can develop a bitter taste.

You will need a big glass jar with a tight-fitting lid to store your liqueur while it is steeping. I like to use half-gallon mason jars, which can be found at most hardware stores for less than ten dollars. Once your liqueur is ready, you will need cheesecloth to strain it and a small funnel to transfer it to a large decanter or divide it between smaller, giftable bottles. The website lunabazaar.com has beautiful, inexpensive bottles that are perfect for filling with delicious, boozy treats.

Simple Syrup

Many of the recipes in this chapter call for a few cups of simple syrup, a basic combination of sugar and water simmered together until the sugar dissolves. You can make a big batch and stash it in the fridge for months—it's a nice thing to have on hand for whipping up cocktails and homemade sodas. You can also make flavored simple syrups by adding slices of fresh ginger, seeded jalapeños, strips of lemon or orange zest, or cinnamon sticks to the saucepan along with the sugar and water.

Makes about 3 cups

2 cups granulated sugar

2 cups water

Combine the sugar and water in a saucepan over medium-low heat. Simmer, stirring, until the sugar dissolves. Cool the syrup completely before adding it to drinks.

Lemony Sweet Tea Vodka

The best thing about this recipe is that it can be made in one hour from start to finish, with incredibly inexpensive ingredients, and the results are far superior to any store-bought sweet tea vodka. Who knew it was so easy? I use Lipton tea because I like its classic, lemony flavor, but feel free to use any black tea you have on hand. On a hot summer day, there is absolutely nothing more refreshing than a boozy Arnold Palmer made with this sweet tea vodka and lemonade. To give this vodka as a hostess gift, pour it into a mason jar and tie a piece of gingham fabric around the lid with kitchen twine.

MAKES ABOUT 8 CUPS

6 cups vodka

6 black tea bags

2 cups simple syrup

2 large, juicy lemons

Pour 3 cups of vodka into each of two 1-quart mason jars. Add 3 tea bags to each jar. Screw on the lids and allow the vodka to stand undisturbed for 1 hour.

Remove the tea bags (be sure to squeeze out all the vodka and add it back to the jars!). Add 1 cup of simple syrup and the juice of one lemon to each jar. Screw on the lids and give the vodka a good shake.

The vodka will keep for up to a year, stored in a cool, dark place.

Pineapple-Mango Tequila

When I first moved to New York at the age of twenty-two, my roommates and I used to frequent a bar on the Upper West Side that was known for their cheap, enormous frozen margaritas. It was by no means a classy joint—the margaritas were dispensed from giant Slurpee machines and served in plastic cups. But we were broke, and our apartment didn't have air-conditioning. That summer we passed many an evening sipping syrupy sweet, fruity margaritas and sharing platters of greasy-yet-delicious fried calamari.

While this tequila hints at the margaritas of my youth, it is a much more sophisticated affair. The fresh pineapple and mango provide a distinctly tropical flavor without being overly sugary. I include one cup of simple syrup but you can leave it out all together if you prefer. To make a simple, refreshing cocktail, pour two ounces of this tequila into a glass with ice, and top with ginger beer and a squeeze of fresh lime.

MAKES ABOUT 4 CUPS

2 cups chopped fresh pineapple

2 cups chopped fresh mango

4 cups white tequila

1 cup simple syrup (optional)

Combine the pineapple and mango, along with any accumulated juices, in a large glass container with a tight-fitting lid. Pour in the tequila, seal the container, and put it in a cool, dark, dry place (like the back of a closet) for 2 weeks. Shake the container every few days.

After 2 weeks, add the simple syrup if using. Reseal the container and let it rest for another 2 weeks, shaking occasionally.

Line a fine mesh sieve with cheesecloth. Pour the liqueur through the sieve and into a large pitcher. Discard any solids. Transfer the liqueur to 1 large or several small bottles. It will keep for a year in a cool, dark place.

Strawberry-Watermelon Rum

I love daiquiris—both the sweet, frozen kind you slurp down poolside, and the classic cocktail made from nothing but rum, lime juice, and a little sugar all shaken together and served up. This summery infused rum is perfect for mixing up daiquiris that combine the best aspects of both drinks. The strawberries and watermelon add bold, fruity flavor without the need for loads of extra sugar. For each drink, combine two ounces of Strawberry-Watermelon Rum, one ounce of freshly squeezed lime juice, and one tablespoon of simple syrup in a cocktail shaker filled with ice. Shake and strain into a martini glass.

MAKES ABOUT 4 CUPS

1 ½ cups cubed watermelon

1 ½ cups washed, hulled, and sliced strawberries

1 (750ml) bottle white rum

1 cup simple syrup, or to taste

Combine the watermelon, strawberries, and rum in a large glass container with a tight-fitting lid. Put the container in a cool, dry, dark place (like the back of a closet) and let it rest for 2 weeks, shaking once after 1 week.

Add the simple syrup and let it rest for 2 more weeks.

Line a fine mesh sieve with cheesecloth. Pour the liqueur through the sieve and into a large pitcher. Discard any solids. Transfer the liqueur to 1 large or several small bottles. It will keep for a year in a cool, dark place.

Raspberry-Lime Liqueur

Across the street from my elementary school was a general store that made the most delicious raspberry-lime rickeys. We used to sneak through the fence at recess to buy huge Styrofoam cups filled with the insanely sweet, fizzy soda. Unfortunately, the teachers usually caught us—our bright red tongues were a dead giveaway! This liqueur recreates the flavors I loved as a child, but with a decidedly more adult twist. It's great for sipping on its own, or try it mixed with sparkling wine or club soda.

MAKES ABOUT 8 CUPS

3 (6-ounce) packages fresh
   raspberries (about 4 cups)

4 cups vodka

$^3/_4$ cup freshly squeezed
   lime juice (about 3 large,
   juicy limes)

3 cups simple syrup

Combine the raspberries, vodka, and lime juice in a large glass container with a tight-fitting lid. Put the container in a cool, dry, dark place (like the back of a closet) and let it rest for 2 weeks, shaking once after 1 week.

Add the simple syrup and let it rest for 2 more weeks.

Line a fine mesh sieve with cheesecloth. Pour the liqueur through the sieve and into a large pitcher. Discard any solids. Transfer the liqueur to 1 large or several small bottles. The liqueur will keep for up to a year stored in a cool, dark place.

Peachy Bourbon (Homemade Southern Comfort)

I know what you're thinking. Southern Comfort is that fruity, syrupy bourbon you haven't had since freshman year of college, right? But before you turn the page, hear me out. My version is made with ripe, juicy peaches, fresh lemon zest, and spicy cinnamon. Add the simple syrup if you want to make more of a sweet, after-dinner liqueur, perfect for sipping on its own. If not, omit it for a more assertive drink. Either way it's delicious mixed with lemonade or ginger ale. This is a great gift to give around Labor Day, because the peaches are reminiscent of summer, while the warming bourbon hints at the crisp, chilly weather ahead.

Makes about 8 cups

1 1/2 pounds fresh, ripe peaches
(about 4 large peaches)

4 cups bourbon

Zest of 1 fresh lemon,
cut into strips

2 to 3 cups simple syrup
(optional)

2 cinnamon sticks

Coarsely chop the peaches and place them, along with any accumulated juices, in a large glass container with a tight-fitting lid. Add the bourbon and lemon zest. Seal the jar and put it in a cool, dark, dry place (like the back of a closet) for 2 weeks. Shake the container every few days.

After 2 weeks, add the simple syrup, if using. Reseal the container and let it rest for 1 more week, shaking occasionally. After 3 weeks, add the cinnamon sticks and let it rest for 1 week more.

Line a fine mesh sieve with cheesecloth. Pour the bourbon through the sieve and into a large pitcher. Discard the cinnamon sticks, lemon zest, and any other solids. Transfer the bourbon to 1 large or several small bottles. It will keep for a year in a cool, dark place.

Cucumber-Jalapeño Vodka

This spicy, refreshing vodka is sure to become your go-to choice for Bloody Marys. I also like to use it in a simple vodka tonic, garnished with a sprig of fresh basil. If you prefer, you can omit the jalapeños and just make a cool, herbaceous cucumber vodka.

MAKES ABOUT 3½ CUPS

½ a hothouse cucumber,
   sliced into rounds

1 (750ml) bottle vodka

2 fresh jalapeño peppers,
   seeded and cut into quarters

Put the cucumber slices into a clean glass jar with a tight-fitting lid. Pour in the vodka. Seal the jar and store it in a cool, dark place, like the back of a closet, for 10 days, shaking occasionally. Add the jalapeño slices and let the vodka rest for 2 more days.

Line a fine mesh sieve with cheesecloth. Pour the vodka through the sieve and into a large pitcher. Discard the cucumber and jalapeño slices. Transfer the vodka to 1 large or several small bottles. It will keep for a year in a cool, dark place.

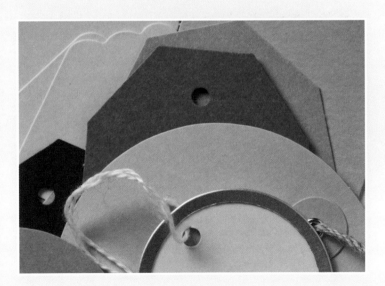

Spiced Pear Gin

In the late fall, when pears come into season, I always buy a whole bunch of firm ones for our kitchen fruit bowl. Then I check them obsessively and impatiently each day until they are soft and juicy and perfect for eating. To me, a perfectly ripe pear is a symbol of the harvest season—plump, sweet, and comforting. This gin makes a wonderful gift for Thanksgiving, Christmas, or Hanukkah. The gingery flavor of cardamom is a natural match for pears, but if you don't have any, you could substitute half a vanilla bean. For a festive drink, pour two tablespoons of Spiced Pear Gin into a Champagne flute and top with sparkling wine.

MAKES ABOUT 6 CUPS

3 large, juicy, ripe Bartlett pears, chopped (about 4 cups)

4 cups gin

2 cups simple syrup

1 cinnamon stick

2 teaspoons whole cardamom pods

3 whole star anise (optional)

Combine the pears, any accumulated juices, and gin in a large glass container with a tight-fitting lid. Put the container in a cool, dry, dark place (like the back of a closet) and let it rest for 2 weeks, shaking once after 1 week.

Add the simple syrup, cinnamon stick, cardamom pods, and star anise (if using) and let it rest for 2 more weeks.

Line a fine mesh sieve with cheesecloth. Pour the liqueur through the sieve and into a large pitcher. Discard any solids. Transfer the liqueur to 1 large or several small bottles. It will keep for a year in a cool, dark place.

Apple-Cinnamon Bourbon

My husband has been known to sneak a small flask filled with this bourbon into baseball and football stadiums. During the brisk fall months, it can be windy in the stands, and a quick nip really warms you from the inside out.

There's no need to splurge on pricy bourbon for this recipe. The sweet-tart green apples, warm cinnamon, and citrusy orange zest lend great flavor to even bottom-shelf bottles. It's delicious served straight up or on the rocks, but don't be afraid to channel your inner mixologist and experiment. Top it with a splash of sparkling wine, add a shot to a glass of hard cider, or use it to make a spiced up Old Fashioned. I chose not to add any sweetener to this version, but if you want to make more of a dessert sipper, add one to two cups of simple syrup.

MAKES ABOUT 4 CUPS

2 large tart apples, such as Granny Smith

1 (750ml) bottle inexpensive bourbon

Zest of 1 fresh orange, cut into 4 thick strips

1 cinnamon stick

Peel the apples and cut them into quarters. Transfer them, along with any accumulated juices, in a large glass container with a tight-fitting lid. Add the bourbon and orange zest. Seal the jar and put it in a cool, dark, dry place (like the back of a closet) for 1 week. Shake the container every couple of days.

After 1 week, add the cinnamon stick. Reseal the jar and allow it to rest for 1 more week, shaking every couple of days.

Line a fine mesh sieve with cheesecloth. Pour the bourbon through the sieve and into a large pitcher. Discard the cinnamon stick, orange zest, and any other solids. Transfer the bourbon to 1 large or several small bottles. It will keep for a year in a cool, dark place.

Made Especially for You by Mother Nature

For unique gift-wrapping ideas, look to your own backyard. Tie any of the objects below to a box of candy, a bottle of liqueur, or a jar of jam for an unexpected twist.

Pinecones	Anise stars	Holly branches
Autumn leaves	Violets	Rosemary or thyme sprigs
Cinnamon sticks	Cherry blossoms	Seashells

Minty Irish Cream Liqueur

I make this liqueur every year around the holidays. It's just the thing for stirring into hot chocolate or enjoying on its own in front of a roaring fire. For a Southern-inspired version, try substituting bourbon for the Irish whiskey. This recipe can easily be doubled or even tripled (just process it in batches in the blender). Consider making a huge batch and dividing it among small, pretty bottles. Makes a great Christmas gift.

MAKES ABOUT 4 ½ CUPS

1 (14-ounce) can sweetened
  condensed milk

1 cup Irish whiskey

$^2/_3$ cup crème de menthe,
  preferably white, not green

1 cup half-and-half

2 tablespoons chocolate syrup
  or melted semisweet chocolate

1 teaspoon instant espresso
  granules

1 teaspoon pure vanilla extract

Combine the sweetened condensed milk, Irish whiskey, crème de menthe, half-and-half, chocolate syrup, espresso granules, and vanilla extract in a blender. Blend until the mixture is smooth and the ingredients are well combined, 1 to 2 minutes. Pour the liqueur into bottles, seal, and store in the refrigerator for up to a month.

Ginger Liqueur

Sometimes after dinner, particularly in the cold winter months, I love to savor a small glass of Domaine de Canton, the fancy liqueur flavored with ginger, vanilla, and orange blossom honey. It's an expensive treat, so I decided to see if I could make a similar-tasting liqueur for a fraction of the price. I kept the ingredient list short and simple so that the fresh, zingy flavor of the ginger would really shine through. Since this is an elegant liqueur, I like to funnel it into pretty antique apothecary bottles to give as gifts. I always tie a note to each bottle with a few cocktail suggestions. Add a splash to Champagne, or make a French martini with equal parts ginger liqueur and vodka, plus a splash of Grand Marnier.

MAKES ABOUT 6 CUPS

1/2 cup peeled, roughly chopped fresh ginger

4 cups vodka

1 cup simple syrup

1/4 cup honey

1/4 teaspoon vanilla extract

Combine the ginger and vodka in a large glass container with a tight-fitting lid. Put the container in a cool, dry, dark place (like the back of a closet) and let it rest for 2 weeks, shaking once after 1 week.

Add the simple syrup, honey, and vanilla and let it rest for 2 more weeks.

Line a fine mesh sieve with cheesecloth. Pour the liqueur through the sieve and into a large pitcher. Discard any solids. Transfer the liqueur to 1 large or several small bottles. It will keep indefinitely in a cool, dark place.

Vin d'Orange

Vin d'Orange (orange wine) is usually made with vodka, but I think brandy makes this elegant aperitif seem even more French. Its flavor is akin to Grand Marnier, but less boozy and with hints of spice from the vanilla and cinnamon. It pairs wonderfully with both cheese and chocolate. Though it's ready to drink as soon as it's strained, Vin d'Orange tastes best after it has rested and mellowed for about a month. I like to decant it in small, pint-sized bottles to give as holiday gifts.

MAKES ABOUT 5 CUPS

2 large navel oranges

1 (750ml) bottle sauvignon blanc

$^1/_2$ cup brandy

$^1/_2$ cup sugar

$^1/_2$ vanilla bean

1 small cinnamon stick

Cut the oranges into quarters and then cut each quarter in half. Put the orange pieces in a large glass container with a tight-fitting lid. Add the wine, brandy, sugar, vanilla bean, and cinnamon stick. Seal the container and let it rest in a cool, dark, dry place (like the back of a closet) for 2 weeks. Shake the container every few days.

Line a fine mesh sieve with cheesecloth. Pour the Vin d'Orange through the sieve and into a large pitcher. Discard any solids. Transfer the Vin d'Orange to bottles and store in the refrigerator for up to a year.

Crema di Limoncello

On a trip to Chicago, my husband and I ate a fantastic meal at the Publican. After feasting on an assortment of artisanal hams, mussels simmered in beer, and a salad topped with crispy fried pigs' ears, there was no way we had room for dessert. Insisting that we must top our dinner off with something sweet, our waiter brought us each a small glass of crema di limoncello. I had never tasted it before, but I fell in love immediately—rich and citrusy, it tasted like melted vanilla ice cream shot through with lemon and booze. This is my approximation of their recipe. For a little added spice, you could include half of a split vanilla bean to the vodka along with the lemon peels.

MAKES ABOUT 7 CUPS

8 large lemons

1 (750ml) bottle vodka

4 cups half-and-half

2 cups sugar

Using a vegetable peeler, peel the zest from the lemons in large strips, being careful not to include any white pith. Discard the lemons or reserve them for another use. Place the peels in a large glass container with a tight-fitting lid. Add the vodka. Seal the jar and put it in a cool, dark, dry place (like the back of a closet) for 2 weeks. Shake the container every few days.

After 2 weeks, combine the half-and-half and sugar in a medium saucepan and heat over medium-low heat, stirring constantly, just until the sugar dissolves. Do not boil. Allow the sugar mixture to cool completely.

Meanwhile, line a fine mesh sieve with cheesecloth. Pour the vodka through the sieve and into a large pitcher. Discard the lemon peels.

Stir the half-and-half into the vodka. Funnel the mixture into 1 large or several small bottles. It will keep for up to a year in the freezer.

Sweet

White Chocolate Fudge with Bourbon and Pecans

Chocolate-Covered Bacon Turtles

Compost Bark

Cinnamon-Raisin Buckeyes

Gingersnap Balls

Peppermint Marshmallows

Maple Syrup Caramels with Fleur de Sel

Chocolate-Covered Pretzel Toffee

Raspberry–Goat Cheese Truffles

Dark Chocolate–Dipped Orangettes

Strawberry Rosé *Pâte de Fruits*

Brandied Cherries

Whiskey Butterscotch Sauce

Chocolate-Hazelnut Almond Spread

Lavender Honey

Pistachio-Honey Butter

Bacon-Chocolate Biscotti

Cornmeal Biscotti with Cranberries, Pecans, and White Chocolate

Maple Walnut Graham Crackers

There is nothing I love more than to spend a leisurely Saturday baking delicious sweet treats like cupcakes, fruity pies, and chocolaty brownies. The only trouble is that I just can't eat them fast enough! Within three or four days, most of my desserts have gone soggy or stale. Plus, gooey, frosted treats are difficult to travel with. Bringing dessert to a party is always a challenge. Once, I nearly cried when I had to transport a cherry crumble on a crowded subway in June, and on more than one occasion, I've had pies collapse and bars get crushed in the backseat of my car.

This chapter is filled with sweets that travel well and last for a while. While there are a few baked treats, such as Maple Walnut Graham Crackers (page 106), Bacon-Chocolate Biscotti (page 103), and Cornmeal Biscotti with Cranberries, Pecans, and White Chocolate (page 104), most of the recipes are for candy. If you've never made candy before, don't fret! These recipes are exceptionally simple and great for beginners. In most cases, you don't need any special equipment (though there are one or two that require a candy thermometer). If you're nervous, start off with something really easy, like Compost Bark (page 82), before moving on to a recipe that is slightly more challenging, like Maple Syrup Caramels with Fleur de Sel (page 88).

One of the things I like best about many of the sweets in this chapter is that they are great for sending in the mail. Biscotti, caramels, graham crackers, fudge, toffee, marshmallows, and orangettes can all be packed tightly in small boxes and dropped in the post with little fear of breakage or spoilage. They make great—and economical—holiday gifts.

White Chocolate Fudge
with Bourbon and Pecans

Purists will tell you that making fudge with marshmallow cream is cheating. But it's so much easier than carefully boiling ingredients to the soft ball stage, and I think the results are just as delicious. You can whip this fudge up in about fifteen minutes, no candy thermometer required. The bourbon adds a hint of oak that compliments the pecans, but you can certainly omit it if you like. Just increase the vanilla to one tablespoon. It will keep for about two weeks, stored in an airtight container at room temperature. This makes a great Christmas gift.

MAKES ABOUT EIGHTY 1-INCH SQUARES OF FUDGE

2 cups sugar

$^2/_3$ cup evaporated milk

6 tablespoons unsalted butter

$^1/_4$ teaspoon kosher salt

1 (7-ounce) jar marshmallow cream

1 (12-ounce) package white chocolate chips

2 tablespoons bourbon

1 teaspoon vanilla extract

1 cup chopped, toasted pecans

Line the bottom and sides of a 9 x 9-inch baking pan with two criss-crossing pieces of aluminum foil, leaving an overhang on each side.

Combine the sugar, evaporated milk, butter, salt, and marshmallow cream in a heavy medium-sized saucepan over medium heat. Stirring constantly, bring the mixture to a boil and cook for 5 minutes.

Remove the saucepan from the heat and add the white chocolate chips, stirring until melted. (You may need to return the pan to low heat to melt the chips completely.) Add the bourbon and vanilla. Stir in the pecans.

Pour the mixture into the prepared pan and allow it to cool to room temperature, about 1 hour. Transfer the pan to the refrigerator and chill for 1 hour.

Using the ends of the foil as handles, lift the fudge out of the pan. Cut the fudge into 1-inch pieces.

Chocolate-Covered Bacon Turtles

Is it possible to improve on the already near-perfect turtle? The combination of crunchy pecans, buttery caramel, and silky chocolate is already about as good as it gets. But adding bacon really pushes the flavor over the top. This recipe is a bit involved because I include instructions for making your own caramel. If you want to cheat and shorten the process, you can use store-bought caramels. Combine them in a bowl with a few tablespoons of milk and heat them in the microwave at one minute intervals until they are melted and smooth. You can pack a whole batch of these turtles in a decorative tin, or drop one or two into cello bags for individual gifts.

MAKES 30 PIECES

$^3/_4$ **pound whole pecan halves (about 3 $^1/_2$ cups)**

5 strips bacon

1 cup heavy cream

5 tablespoons unsalted butter, diced

1 teaspoon vanilla extract

1 $^1/_2$ cups sugar

3 tablespoons light corn syrup

1 (12-ounce) package bittersweet chocolate chips

Preheat the oven to 325°F. Spread the pecans in an even layer on a baking sheet. Bake until the pecans are fragrant and toasted, stirring occasionally, about 6 or 7 minutes. Remove the pecans from the oven and let cool.

Fry the bacon in a large skillet until very crisp, about 8 minutes. Transfer the bacon to a paper towel–lined plate and let cool. When the bacon is cool enough to handle, cut each strip into 6 pieces with kitchen shears. Set the bacon pieces aside.

Line 2 baking sheets with parchment paper. Arrange the pecans in star-shaped clusters of five. You should have enough whole pecan halves to make 30 clusters. (If you don't, you can arrange broken pieces into little piles. They won't look like turtles, but they will still be delicious.) Set the baking sheets aside.

In a small saucepan, combine the heavy cream, butter, and vanilla extract. Bring it to a boil over medium heat, then immediately remove from the heat.

In a medium saucepan, combine the sugar, corn syrup, and $^1/_4$ cup of water. Bring it to a boil over medium-high heat, stirring until the sugar is dissolved. Reduce the heat to a simmer and cook the

sugar mixture, without stirring, but swirling the pan occasionally, until it begins to turn golden-amber in color, about 6 to 8 minutes.

Reduce the heat to medium-low. Very carefully, pour the hot cream mixture into the sugar mixture. It will bubble ferociously. Stir until combined. Clip a candy thermometer to the side of the pan and cook, stirring occasionally, until the mixture reaches 248°F (firm ball stage), 10 to 15 minutes. Remove the pan from the heat and allow the caramel to cool slightly, about 5 minutes.

Using a soup spoon, drop mounds of caramel into the center of each pecan cluster. Top each with 1 piece of bacon, pressing gently to adhere. (If the caramel becomes too stiff to work with, reheat gently over low heat.) Set the turtles aside to cool, about 45 minutes to 1 hour.

Heat $^2/_3$ of the chocolate chips in a heat-proof bowl set over a pan of simmering water until melted. Remove the bowl from the pan and stir in the remaining third of chocolate chips until melted and smooth.

Using a soup spoon, top each turtle with a spoonful of melted chocolate, smoothing to cover the bacon completely. Set the turtles aside until the chocolate hardens. The turtles will keep for up to 2 weeks, stored between sheets of wax paper in an airtight container at room temperature.

Compost Bark

I have a bit of a culinary crush on Christina Tosi, the pastry chef at Momofuku Milk Bar in New York. She bakes up the craziest, most whimsical creations, my favorite of which is the Compost Cookie. It has a little bit of everything in it, including candy bar bits, potato chips, pretzels, nuts, and chocolate chips. Somehow, instead of tasting like a clumsy mishmash of ingredients, it's the perfect balance of salty and sweet, crunchy and tender. Inspired by Christina's innovative use of potato chips, I created this chocolate bark. Play around with the ingredient combinations. It would also be delicious with corn flakes and tortilla chips.

MAKES ABOUT 1 POUND

1 pound (16 ounces) semisweet chocolate, chopped

1 cup puffed rice cereal, such as Rice Krispies

1 cup crushed gourmet-style potato chips

1 cup crushed pretzels

Line a large baking sheet with parchment paper.

Melt the chocolate in a heatproof bowl set over a pan of simmering water, stirring frequently. When the chocolate has melted completely, remove the bowl from the heat and stir in the cereal, potato chips, and pretzels.

Pour the mixture onto the prepared baking sheet, spreading it to roughly $1/2$-inch thickness. Let the bark cool at room temperature until it is hard and set, about 3 or 4 hours. Break the bark into large chunks. It will keep for about a month stored in an airtight container at room temperature, or in the refrigerator if the weather is warm.

Cinnamon-Raisin Buckeyes

I am obsessed with Peanut Butter & Co.'s Cinnamon Raisin Swirl peanut butter. Spread on a piece of toast (or, if we're being completely honest here, spooned straight from the jar), it tastes like nutty, spicy heaven. One day I had the genius idea to incorporate the same flavors into a recipe for traditional buckeyes. Famous especially in Ohio, buckeyes are peanut butter balls dipped in chocolate, resembling the nut of a buckeye tree. You will need a bunch of toothpicks to dip the balls part way into the melted chocolate. Since the balls of dough need plenty of time to firm up, it's best to start preparing these a day in advance. These are great to take along to a Super Bowl party.

MAKES ABOUT 40 BUCKEYES

1/2 cup raisins

2 cups creamy peanut butter

1/4 pound (1 stick) unsalted butter, softened

2 1/2 cups confectioners' sugar

1 1/4 cups graham cracker crumbs

1/2 teaspoon cinnamon

10 ounces semisweet chocolate, chopped

Pulse the raisins in a food processor until they are coarsely chopped. Transfer them to a large bowl and add the peanut butter and butter. Beat with an electric mixer until the mixture is combined and softened, about 1 to 2 minutes. Beat in the confectioners' sugar, graham cracker crumbs, and cinnamon. The mixture will be a bit stiff and crumbly.

Roll the dough into 1-inch balls and place them on a parchment-lined baking sheet. Chill the balls in the refrigerator overnight.

The next day, melt the chocolate in a heat-proof bowl set over a pan of gently simmering water. Remove the balls from the refrigerator and spear each one with a toothpick. Dip the balls two-thirds of the way into the chocolate. Return the balls to the baking sheet and chill until the chocolate has set, about 1 hour. Remove the toothpicks. Store the buckeyes in an airtight container in the refrigerator for up to 10 days.

Gingersnap Balls

These Gingersnap Balls are a great, no-bake holiday treat. I love the flavor combination of spicy ginger, nutty walnuts, and sweet dark rum. They are a cinch to make and the results are so fancy looking, no one will ever guess you used supermarket gingersnap cookies. For simplicity's sake, I usually roll my balls in extra gingersnap crumbs, but you could use ground nuts or cocoa powder, or dip them in melted chocolate.

MAKES ABOUT 30 BALLS

About 45 store-bought gingersnap cookies, such as Nabisco

1 1/2 cups walnuts

1 cup confectioners' sugar

1/2 teaspoon ground ginger

2 tablespoons maple syrup, honey, or corn syrup

1/3 cup dark rum

Working in batches, put the gingersnaps in the work bowl of a food processor and process until they are finely ground. You should have about 3 cups of crumbs. Transfer 2 cups to a large bowl. Reserve the remaining 1 cup of crumbs. Put the walnuts in the food processor and process until they are finely ground. Add them to the bowl with the 2 cups of gingersnap crumbs. Add the confectioners' sugar and ground ginger and stir until well combined. Stir in the maple syrup and rum. Transfer the mixture to the refrigerator and chill for 30 minutes.

Spread the remaining cup of gingersnap crumbs on a plate. Using a tablespoon, scoop out spoonfuls of the mixture and shape them into 1-inch balls. Roll the balls in the gingersnap crumbs. Transfer them to a wax paper–lined baking sheet and chill until they are set, about 1 hour. Store the balls in an airtight container in the refrigerator for up to 2 weeks.

Peppermint Marshmallows

On a winter vacation in Banff National Park, my husband and I spent many evenings in the lobby of our hotel, lounging in front of a roaring fire, fingers curled around mugs of hot chocolate spiked with peppermint schnapps. I returned home determined to create a peppermint marshmallow perfect for topping off hot cocoa. You can also use them to make delicious minty s'mores.

Homemade marshmallows are easy as pie to make, but they do require a bit of patience. You have to beat the ingredients for about ten minutes to create a thick, glossy fluff. I usually set a kitchen timer and page through a magazine with one hand. Once poured into the pan, the marshmallow mixture needs to set for several hours. I suggest leaving it uncovered on the counter overnight. If you must cover it, make sure the plastic wrap or aluminum foil doesn't touch the surface of the marshmallows. It will stick and stick hard.

Makes 30 to 40 marshmallows

Confectioners' sugar for dusting

3 envelopes unflavored gelatin

2 cups sugar

$1/2$ cup light corn syrup

$1/4$ teaspoon kosher salt

2 large egg whites

1 tablespoon peppermint schnapps

Spray a 13 x 9-inch baking pan with nonstick spray and dust it with confectioners' sugar.

Pour $1/2$ cup of cold water into a large bowl and sprinkle the gelatin over it. Let it stand to soften.

Combine the sugar, corn syrup, salt, and $1/2$ cup of water in a medium-sized, heavy saucepan. Clip a candy thermometer to the side and heat over low heat, stirring until the sugar dissolves. Increase the heat to medium and boil, without stirring, until the mixture reaches 240°F, about 10 minutes.

Pour the sugar mixture into the bowl with the gelatin and stir until the gelatin is completely dissolved. Using an electric mixer, beat the sugar mixture until it is thick, shiny, and tripled in volume. Be patient—this will take about 10 minutes.

Wash and dry the beaters. In a separate large bowl, beat the egg whites until they hold stiff peaks. Beat the egg whites and the peppermint schnapps into the sugar mixture. Pour the mixture into the prepared pan.

Let the pan stand for at least 4 hours and preferably overnight, uncovered or loosely covered with the plastic wrap or aluminum foil not touching the surface of the marshmallows, until the marshmallow is set. To cut the marshmallow, dust a cutting board with confectioners' sugar. Dust the surface of the marshmallow with confectioners' sugar. Invert the pan over the cutting board. Using your fingers, carefully wiggle the marshmallow out of the pan. Cut the marshmallow into squares and dust them with more confectioners' sugar. Store them in an airtight container for up to a week.

Maple Syrup Caramels with Fleur de Sel

These caramels are salty, chewy, and full of pure maple sweetness. I like to make them in the fall and give them to friends around Halloween and Thanksgiving. Grade B maple syrup will give the caramels a more pronounced flavor, but if you can only find grade A, that will work fine, too. You can omit the fleur de sel if you don't have any on hand; just increase the kosher salt to ³/₄ teaspoon.

To wrap the caramels, cut three- to four-inch squares of wax paper. Roll each caramel in a square of the paper and twist the ends to seal them shut. To get a little fancy, tie a tiny piece of ribbon to each end.

Makes about 40 caramels

1 cup heavy cream

5 tablespoons unsalted butter, diced

¹/₂ teaspoon sea salt

¹/₂ teaspoon maple extract (optional)

1 cup sugar

¹/₂ cup pure maple syrup

3 tablespoons light corn syrup

¹/₄ cup water

1 teaspoon fleur de sel

Line the bottom of an 8 x 8-inch square baking pan with aluminum foil, leaving an overhang on two sides. Line the pan again with parchment paper, leaving an overhang on the opposite sides from the foil. Lightly oil the parchment or spray it with nonstick spray. Set aside.

Combine the heavy cream, butter, salt, and maple extract (if using) in a small saucepan and bring it to a boil, then remove the saucepan from the heat and set aside.

Combine the sugar, maple syrup, corn syrup, and water in a large saucepan. Bring it to a boil over medium heat, stirring until the sugar dissolves. Once the sugar dissolves, boil without stirring, but swirling the pan occasionally, for 6 minutes. (The mixture will darken slightly, from golden to amber.)

Carefully pour the cream mixture into the sugar mixture. It will bubble vigorously. Reduce the heat to medium-low and simmer until a candy thermometer registers 248°F. Pour the caramel into the prepared pan and sprinkle with the fleur de sel. Allow the caramel to cool for at least 3 hours. Cut the caramel into 1-inch pieces (using clean kitchen scissors makes this task really easy) and wrap the pieces in wax paper. The caramels will keep for at least a week stored in an airtight container at room temperature, and even longer in the refrigerator.

Candy Wrapping

Most well-stocked craft stores have a wide selection of boxes, bags, and tins for packaging candy and other homemade treats. Here are some ideas for dressing them up.

- Use rubber stamps to decorate plain white candy boxes. Line the boxes with pieces of colored tissue paper.

- Glue paper doilies to brown paper sandwich bags.

- Repurpose small boxes and jars by painting them and gluing photos to the lids.

- Use name tags to label gifts. "Hello. My Name is Chocolate-Covered Pretzel Toffee."

- Get creative with strips of fabric, beads, buttons, bells, ribbon, newspaper, and clean Chinese food takeout containers.

Chocolate-Covered Pretzel Toffee

This toffee is sort of like a nut brittle, only with pretzels in place of the nuts and a more intense butter flavor. Oh, and did I mention it's covered in chocolate? If you're a salt fiend like me, sprinkle it with a little fleur de sel at the end.

Make sure you use thin pretzels in this recipe. The thicker ones are too bulky and don't have enough salt or flavor. You can crush them by hand, with a large butcher knife, or pulse them a few times in the food processor.

This toffee travels exceptionally well, so it's perfect for mailing to far-flung friends.

MAKES ABOUT 1 POUND

$^1/_4$ **pound (1 stick) unsalted butter, at room temperature**

1 $^1/_4$ cups sugar

1 tablespoon light corn syrup

$^1/_4$ teaspoon kosher salt

$^1/_4$ teaspoon baking soda

$^1/_2$ teaspoon vanilla extract

1 $^1/_2$ cups crushed thin pretzel twists or thin pretzel sticks

6 ounces semisweet chocolate chips

1 teaspoon fleur de sel or other flaky sea salt (optional)

Line a baking sheet with parchment paper. Set aside.

Combine the butter, sugar, corn syrup, salt, and 2 tablespoons of water in a medium-sized heavy saucepan. Clip a candy thermometer to the side of the pan and cook over medium heat, gently stirring occasionally, until the thermometer reaches 300°F (hard crack stage), about 10 minutes.

Remove the saucepan from the heat and immediately stir in the baking soda and vanilla extract. Stir in the crushed pretzels.

Quickly pour the toffee onto the prepared baking sheet, spreading it as thinly and evenly as possible. Let the toffee cool slightly until it just begins to harden, about 3 minutes. Sprinkle it evenly with the chocolate chips. Let it stand until the chocolate has melted, about 2 minutes. Using a spatula, spread the chocolate evenly over the toffee. Sprinkle the chocolate with fleur de sel if using.

Transfer the baking sheet to the refrigerator and chill until the chocolate has hardened, about 2 hours. Break the toffee into large shards. Store in an airtight container for up to 3 weeks.

Raspberry–
Goat Cheese Truffles

Chocolate and goat cheese may seem like a bit of an odd couple, but the flavor combination is unexpectedly delicious—sweet, tangy, and intensely creamy. Because raspberries pair magnificently with both chocolate and goat cheese, I included some raspberry jam. Strawberry, fig, or blueberry jam would be delicious, too. If you can't find thin chocolate wafer cookies (I use Nabisco), you can substitute chocolate graham crackers.

MAKES ABOUT 30 TRUFFLES

12 ounces bittersweet chocolate, chopped

2 (3.5-ounce) packages fresh soft goat cheese, room temperature

$^1/_4$ cup confectioners' sugar

3 tablespoons raspberry jam

1 cup finely crushed chocolate wafer cookies, such as Nabisco

Melt the chocolate in a heatproof bowl set over a pan of simmering water, stirring until smooth. Allow the chocolate to cool slightly, about 20 minutes.

Combine the goat cheese, confectioners' sugar, and jam in a large bowl. Beat with an electric mixer until the mixture is light and fluffy, about 2 minutes. Add the cooled chocolate and beat until well combined. Transfer the mixture to the refrigerator and chill until it is firm, about 1 to 2 hours.

Spread the chocolate cookie crumbs on a plate. Form scant tablespoons of the chocolate mixture into balls and roll them in the cookie crumbs. Store the truffles in the refrigerator, in an airtight container, separated by sheets of parchment or wax paper, for up to 10 days. Once removed from the fridge, they will hold up well at room temperature for several hours.

I love you.

Dark Chocolate–Dipped Orangettes

I'm the kind of person who freezes the rinds of Parmesan cheese for soup, makes croutons out of stale bread, and gets every last bit of peanut butter out of the jar (and then repurposes the jar as a salad dressing container). So naturally, I love orangettes, otherwise known as candied orange peel. Not only are they *très* French, they're also *très* economical, and a great way to use up something that would normally end up in the trash can. For this recipe I recommend using the darkest chocolate you can find. I like Lindt® Excellence 85% Cocoa Extra Dark. You will end up with about 100 orangettes, which is enough for four or five small gifts. I like to team them up with small bags of My Nana's Buttered Almonds (page 34).

Makes about 100 orangettes

6 medium navel oranges

4 cups sugar, plus more for coating

7 ounces (two 3.5-ounce bars) dark chocolate, preferably 85%, chopped

1 teaspoon orange or almond liqueur (optional)

Slice the tops and bottoms off each orange. Score the remaining peel into quarters. Remove each peel in 4 strips. Reserve the oranges for another use. Cut the strips lengthwise into $1/4$-inch slices.

Put the orange peels in a medium saucepan and add cold water to cover. Bring to a boil over medium heat. Pour off the water. Repeat 1 or 2 more times.

Combine 4 cups of sugar and 1 cup of water in a large saucepan. Bring to a simmer, and simmer for 10 minutes. Add the orange peels and continue to simmer until the peels are slightly translucent, about 45 minutes. Drain the peels and toss them with sugar to coat. Let the peels dry on a wire rack for 6 to 8 hours, or overnight.

Place the chocolate in a heatproof bowl set over a pan of simmering water. Heat, stirring frequently, until the chocolate has melted. Remove the bowl from heat and stir in the liqueur, if using.

Dip each orange peel halfway in the chocolate. Transfer the peels to the wire rack and allow them to stand until the chocolate has hardened, 2 to 3 hours. Store the orangettes in an airtight container at room temperature for up to 2 weeks.

Strawberry Rosé *Pâte de Fruits*

I have been to Paris twice with my father. He is an art historian, and I am a food writer, and so we could never agree on what to do! All he wanted was to wander through the Louvre, and all I wanted was to eat my way through the city's fanciest cheese shops and pâtisseries. One of my favorite French treats were *pâte de fruits*, or fruit jellies, which glitter like jewels and taste incredibly sweet and delicate. For this recipe, I love to pair a dry French rosé with strawberry jam, but feel free to play with different flavor combinations. Champagne and raspberries would be divine. To give these as a gift, place each candy in a paper or foil mini-muffin wrapper and arrange them in a pretty tin.

MAKES ABOUT 30 CANDIES

$^2/_3$ **cup dry rosé wine, divided**

2 envelopes unflavored gelatin

1 $^1/_4$ cups sugar, divided

1 cup seedless strawberry jam

Line an 8-inch square pan with parchment paper and spray it with nonstick spray. Set aside.

Pour $^1/_3$ cup of the wine into a small bowl and sprinkle with the gelatin. Let it stand until softened, about 5 minutes.

Combine the remaining $^1/_3$ cup of wine and $^3/_4$ cup of the sugar in a medium saucepan over medium heat. Stir until the sugar dissolves and the mixture reaches a boil. Add the jam and stir until it melts and the mixture is smooth. Add the softened gelatin and stir until smooth. Bring the mixture back to boil and boil for 2 minutes.

Pour the mixture into the prepared pan. Let it cool to room temperature, about 1 hour, and then transfer it to the refrigerator. Chill until it is set, about 4 hours.

Pour the remaining $^1/_2$ cup of sugar into a small, shallow bowl. Using a sharp knife, cut the candy into small squares. Roll each square in the sugar, making sure to coat all sides.

Store the *pâte de fruits* in layers separated by wax or parchment paper in an airtight container for up to 3 weeks. You may need to dust with sugar again before serving.

Brandied Cherries

As a little girl, the first thing I did when presented with an ice cream sundae was to pluck the maraschino cherry from the top and cast it aside with a resounding *yuck*. Rest assured that these boozy cherries are nothing like their neon-hued, artificial tasting counterparts! You can use them in desserts, or as a cocktail garnish. Once the cherries are gone, the infused brandy makes a delicious after dinner drink.

4 CUPS, OR 4 HALF-PINT JARS

2 cups brandy

1 $^1/_2$ cups packed brown sugar

$^1/_4$ teaspoon nutmeg

4 cups fresh sweet cherries (do not pit or stem)

4 cinnamon sticks

Combine the brandy, brown sugar, and nutmeg in a medium saucepan and bring to a simmer over medium-low heat. Simmer, stirring frequently, just until the sugar dissolves.

Divide the cherries evenly between 4 clean, hot half-pint jars. Tuck a cinnamon stick into each jar. Pour the brandy mixture into the jars over the cherries, making sure to cover the cherries completely (add a bit more brandy if needed). Seal the jars and transfer them to the refrigerator to marinate for 1 week.

The cherries will keep in the refrigerator for up to a month.

Happy Birthday!

Happy Birthday!

Brandied Cherries

HAPPY BIRTHDAY TO YOU!

Whiskey Butterscotch Sauce

Store-bought butterscotch sauce is often gluey and cloyingly sweet. It usually tastes of little more than artificial caramel. Real homemade butterscotch sauce, on the other hand, is a marvelous combination of flavors including brown sugar, butter, salt, and whiskey. The best part? It takes less than thirty minutes to make and all you need is a pot, a wooden spoon, and some jars. It goes without saying that this is fantastic over ice cream, but try it with bread pudding, waffles, and pancakes, too. A jar makes a great gift for St. Patrick's Day.

MAKES ABOUT 2 CUPS, OR 2 HALF-PINT JARS

- 1 $^1/_2$ cups packed light brown sugar

- $^1/_3$ cup light corn syrup

- 2 tablespoons unsalted butter

- 1 teaspoon flaky sea salt, such as fleur de sel

- $^3/_4$ cup heavy cream

- 3 tablespoons whiskey

- $^1/_2$ teaspoon vanilla extract

Combine the light brown sugar, corn syrup, butter, salt, and $^1/_4$ cup of water in a medium-sized heavy pot. Bring to a simmer and cook until the sugar dissolves, 2 to 3 minutes. Add the cream and continue to simmer until the sauce is thick and syrupy, about 12 minutes. Stir in the whiskey and vanilla extract. Simmer for 3 more minutes. Allow the sauce to cool to room temperature, about 40 minutes, then transfer it to 2 clean half-pint jars. The sauce will keep for up to a month in the refrigerator.

Chocolate-Hazelnut Almond Spread

I've admired Susan Herrmann Loomis since my first job out of college, as a fledgling assistant in the cookbook division of a major publishing house. Who wouldn't? Following her passion for all things French and farmhouse, she moved from the United States to Normandy, where she lives in a converted monastery and runs a highly acclaimed cooking school. *Sigh*. Maybe someday.

Susan's cookbook, *Nuts in the Kitchen*, has a fantastic recipe for chocolate hazelnut spread. Imagine a slightly chunky, less sweet, grown-up version of Nutella. I set out to make it one day only to discover that I didn't have enough hazelnuts. I improvised by adding almonds, and ended up liking my improvised version even better than the original. This recipe makes an ideal gift for anyone who is nuts about chocolate.

MAKES ABOUT 1½ CUPS, OR THREE 4-OUNCE JARS

1 cup hazelnuts

1 cup almonds

³/₄ cup confectioners' sugar

¹/₄ cup best quality cocoa powder, such as Valrhona

Pinch of kosher salt

3 tablespoons canola oil

Preheat the oven to 375°F. Spread the hazelnuts on one side of a baking sheet and the almonds on the other. Toast the nuts until they are fragrant, about 8 to 10 minutes.

Remove the baking sheet from the oven and transfer the hazelnuts to a clean kitchen towel. Scrub and roll them around until most of the skins come off. Don't worry if you don't get all the skins off—just do the best you can.

Combine the hazelnuts and almonds in a food processor and process until they make a smooth paste, about 5 minutes. Add the confectioners' sugar, cocoa powder, and salt and process until the ingredients are well blended.

With the processor running, pour in the canola oil and continue to process until it is well incorporated.

Transfer the Chocolate-Hazelnut Almond Spread to three 4-ounce jars. It will keep for up to a month in the refrigerator.

Lavender Honey

The uses for this elegant, fragrant honey are endless. Drizzle it over scones, stir it into iced tea or lemonade, or use it to bake delicious shortbread. Dried lavender buds can be found at some farmers' markets, specialty spice shops, and online. It might take a little sleuthing to get your hands on it, but it is well worth the effort. If you have never cooked with lavender before, you're in for a treat.

MAKES ABOUT 2 CUPS, OR 2 HALF-PINT JARS

2 cups mild honey, such as clover

$^1/_4$ cup dried lavender buds

2 strips fresh orange peel

Combine the honey, lavender buds, and orange peels in a medium saucepan and heat over low heat, stirring occasionally, for 30 minutes. Pour the honey through a fine mesh sieve into a large bowl and discard the solids. Transfer the honey to 2 clean half-pint jars and store for up to a year at room temperature.

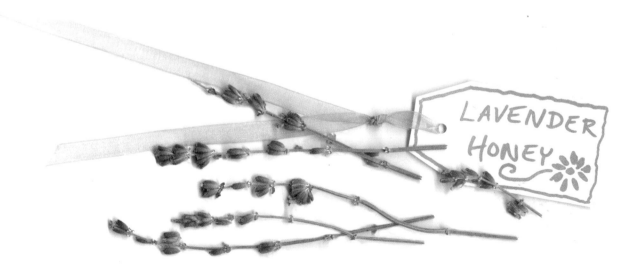

Pistachio-Honey Butter

There is a fancy gourmet market in my neighborhood that sells the most delicious pistachio butter. Brilliant green, slightly sweet, and intensely nutty, it's easily one of the best spreads I have ever eaten. The trouble is, it's imported from Italy and costs $30 a jar. Since I just can't live without it slathered on my morning toast, I decided to see if I could create a homemade version. This butter is every bit as addictive as the fancy store-bought version. The pistachios are rich and nutty, and the honey adds a mild, floral sweetness. The consistency is smooth and slightly granular, with tiny nuggets of pistachio throughout.

MAKES 1 1/2 CUPS
(THREE 4-OUNCE JARS)

1 cup raw, shelled pistachios

1 cup whole blanched almonds

1/2 teaspoon kosher salt

1/4 cup honey

3 tablespoons vegetable oil

Preheat the oven to 375°F. Spread the pistachios and almonds on a baking sheet. Toast the nuts until fragrant, about 7 or 8 minutes.

Transfer the nuts to a food processor fitted with the blade attachment. Process until nuts "melt" into a smooth paste, about 8 to 10 minutes. You may need to stop the processor once or twice to scrape down the sides of the bowl.

Add the salt and honey and process until well blended. With the processor running, slowly drizzle in the oil. Continue to process until the oil is well incorporated and smooth, about 7 or 8 minutes more. Transfer the pistachio butter to jars and store in the refrigerator for up to 2 months.

Bacon-Chocolate Biscotti

The rich chocolate chunks in these biscotti are the perfect complement to the salty, meaty bacon. Chopping the bacon in the food processor may seem a bit fussy, but trust me—the tiny bits infuse every last crumb with smoky, bacon-y deliciousness. Each bite yields layer upon layer of mostly-sweet-but-also-savory flavors. For an extra nutty crunch, toss in a handful of chopped pecans. These biscotti are absolutely divine dunked in your morning coffee. They will keep for three weeks, stored in an airtight container.

MAKES ABOUT 3 DOZEN BISCOTTI

5 strips bacon

2 cups all-purpose flour

1 $^1/_4$ teaspoons baking powder

$^1/_4$ teaspoon kosher salt

$^1/_4$ pound (1 stick) unsalted butter, softened

$^3/_4$ cup sugar

2 large eggs

6 ounces semisweet chocolate chips (about 1 cup)

Fry the bacon in a skillet until browned and crisp, about 5 minutes. Transfer to a paper towel–lined plate to drain. Allow the bacon to cool completely. Transfer the bacon to a food processor and pulse until it is coarsely chopped. Set aside.

Whisk the flour, baking powder, and salt in a medium bowl. In a large bowl, beat the butter and sugar with an electric mixer until it is light and fluffy, 2 or 3 minutes. Add the eggs one at a time and beat to combine. Add the flour mixture and beat until blended. Stir in the bacon and chocolate chips. Gather the dough into a ball and divide in half. Wrap each half in plastic and refrigerate until firm, 20 to 30 minutes.

Line a baking sheet with parchment paper. Preheat the oven to 350°F. On a floured surface, roll each piece of dough out into a 12- to 14-inch log. Transfer the logs to the baking sheet and space them 3 to 4 inches apart. Bake them until they are light golden and dry to the touch, about 30 minutes.

Remove the baking sheet from the oven. Reduce the oven temperature to 300°F. Allow the logs to cool for 15 minutes. Transfer the logs to the cutting board. Using a serrated knife, slice the logs on a diagonal into $^1/_2$-inch thick slices. Return the slices to the baking sheet, standing upright, and bake them until they are dry and golden, 20 to 30 minutes.

Cornmeal Biscotti with Cranberries, Pecans, and White Chocolate

The cornmeal in these biscotti makes them extra crunchy and gives them a slightly nutty, toasty flavor. You can play around with the combination of fruit, nuts, and chocolate. Try dried cherries, almonds, and dark chocolate, or omit the fruit and make them with pistachios and milk chocolate. Biscotti is traditionally served with vin santo, a fancy Italian dessert wine. But I like to munch on these while sipping a märzen (aka Oktoberfest) beer. Arrange these biscotti in a pretty tin and pair them with a six-pack for a terrific fall hostess gift.

MAKES ABOUT 3 DOZEN BISCOTTI

1 cup all-purpose flour

1 cup yellow cornmeal

1 teaspoon baking powder

$^1/_4$ teaspoon kosher salt

$^3/_4$ cup sugar

$^1/_4$ pound (1 stick) unsalted butter, softened

2 large eggs

2 teaspoons vanilla extract

$^3/_4$ cup dried cranberries

$^3/_4$ cup chopped, toasted pecans

1 (12-ounce) bag white chocolate chips (about 2 cups)

In a medium bowl, whisk together the flour, cornmeal, baking powder, and salt.

Combine the sugar and butter in a large bowl and beat with an electric mixer until light and fluffy, about 2 minutes. Beat in the eggs one at a time and then beat in the vanilla extract. Add the flour mixture and beat just until blended. Stir in the cranberries and the pecans.

Gather the dough together and divide it in half. Wrap each half in plastic wrap and freeze them for 25 minutes. Meanwhile, preheat the oven to 350°F and line a baking sheet with parchment paper.

Lightly flour your hands and form each piece of dough into a log about 14 inches long and $2^1/_2$ inches wide. Transfer the logs to the baking sheet. Bake for 25 minutes, until the logs are puffed and dry. Remove them from the oven and let them cool on the baking sheet for 20 minutes.

Reduce the oven to 225°F. Place the logs on a cutting board and, using a serrated knife, slice them diagonally into $^1/_2$-inch thick slices. Return the slices to the baking sheet, standing them upright. Bake for 20 minutes, until they are dry and crisp at the edges. Cool completely on a wire rack. (Reserve the parchment-lined baking sheet.)

Set a heatproof bowl over a pan of gently simmering water. Add the white chocolate chips to the bowl and heat, stirring occasionally, until they are melted and smooth. Dip the bottom (flat) half of each biscotti in the chocolate and place them back on the baking sheet, cut side down, to dry. The biscotti will keep for up to a month, stored in an airtight container at room temperature.

Maple Walnut Graham Crackers

Nancy Silverton, the celebrated cookbook author and owner of La Brea Bakery in Los Angeles, makes homemade graham crackers that are so delicious, you may never be able to go back to the store-bought kind again. I can never resist playing around with her basic recipe. This variation, spiked with maple syrup and loaded with walnuts, is my favorite. It goes without saying these graham crackers make a superb base for s'mores. I also like them topped with ricotta and drizzled with honey.

MAKES 24 TO 32 (4 X 2-INCH) CRACKERS

1 $^3/_4$ cups all-purpose flour, plus more for dusting

1 cup finely ground walnuts, divided

1 cup lightly packed dark brown sugar

1 teaspoon baking soda

$^3/_4$ teaspoon kosher salt

7 tablespoons unsalted butter, cut into cubes and frozen for 10 minutes

$^1/_3$ cup pure maple syrup

5 tablespoons whole milk

1 teaspoon vanilla extract

1 teaspoon maple extract (optional)

3 tablespoons granulated sugar

$^3/_4$ teaspoon cinnamon

Combine the flour, $^3/_4$ cup of the ground walnuts, brown sugar, baking soda, and salt in a food processor and pulse to blend. Add the butter and pulse until the mixture resembles wet sand.

Combine the maple syrup, milk, vanilla extract, and maple extract (if using) in a small bowl. Add to the flour mixture and pulse just until the dough comes together. It will be very soft and sticky. Scoop the dough onto a large sheet of plastic wrap. Do your best to shape it into a 1-inch-thick rectangle. Wrap the dough in plastic and chill in the refrigerator for at least 2 hours and up to several days.

Line 2 baking sheets with parchment paper. Generously flour the work surface and the rolling pin. Divide the dough in half and return one half to the refrigerator. Roll the dough out into a long, thin rectangle. It will be very soft and sticky; flour as necessary. Trim the edges of the dough and cut the dough into 4 x 2-inch rectangles. Transfer the rectangles to one of the baking sheets. Reroll scraps and cut more rectangles. You should have a total of 12 to 14. Use the tines of a fork to poke 5 rows of holes down the center of each cracker and to crimp the edges. Repeat with the second half of dough.

Combine the remaining $^1/_4$ cup of ground walnuts with the granulated sugar and cinnamon in a small bowl. Sprinkle the mixture evenly over the graham crackers.

Transfer the baking sheets to the refrigerator and chill for 30 minutes. Preheat the oven to 350°F. Bake the crackers until lightly browned around the edges and slightly firm to the touch, about 15 minutes, rotating baking sheets halfway through. Cool the graham crackers completely on the rack, then transfer to an airtight container. They will keep for about 1 week.

Spicy Condiments, Pickles, and Snacks

Lemon Salt with Fennel and Red Pepper Flakes

Lavender Salt

Margarita Salt

Habanero Hot Sauce

Ginger Sriracha

Chipotle Ketchup

Honey-Beer Mustard

Chocolate Barbecue Sauce

Balsamic-Raisin Steak Sauce

Spicy Tomato Confit

Pineapple Salsa

Spicy Marinated Artichoke Hearts

Bread-and-Butter Zucchini Relish

Blue Cheese and Almond-Stuffed Olives

Pickled Fennel

Root Beer Jerky

Dill-Pickled Brussels Sprouts

Before we went to Thailand, my husband and I were warned repeatedly by friends that the food is incredibly hot. "Order everything 'not spicy'—it will still be the hottest thing you've ever eaten," one recommended. Another swore that an especially fiery green papaya salad made her hallucinate! For the most part, we heeded their advice. But one night we let our waitress at the White Orchid Beach Restaurant in Phuket persuade us to order a fish dish "just a little bit spicy—one chile!" It was so hot that I actually wept. I kept eating, though, with tears streaming down my cheeks, because it was also so incredibly delicious. That's the thing about chiles and other hot spices. They add a lot more than just fire to food. They also create layers of complex flavor.

Don't worry. The condiments, pickles, and snacks in this chapter won't make you, or anyone you give them to, cry. Most of them have just a little extra kick from jalapeños, red pepper flakes, chipotle chiles, or chili powder. And a few (such as Bread-and-Butter Zucchini Relish, page 133, and Pickled Fennel, page 136) aren't even spicy in the hot sense; they're simply flavored with heady ingredients like garlic, celery seeds, fresh thyme, and turmeric.

Most people already have a refrigerator door packed with half-empty jars of mustard, Tabasco, and barbecue sauce left over from last summer's Fourth of July

cookout. And while there's nothing really *wrong* with the store-bought stuff, homemade versions are so much fresher and more flavorful. The right condiment or accompaniment can turn a dish from bland to breathtaking. A simple sprinkle of Lemon Salt with Fennel and Red Pepper Flakes (page 116) transforms plain chicken breasts, a slick of Honey-Beer Mustard (page 125) makes your take-to-work ham sandwich pop, and Blue Cheese and Almond-Stuffed Olives (page 134) are the perfect garnish for a dirty martini. Many of the recipes would make great additions to summer picnic parties, like Chipotle Ketchup (page 122), Chocolate Barbecue Sauce (page 126), and Balsamic-Raisin Steak Sauce (page 127), but there are plenty of cold weather treats, too. Honey-Beer Mustard would make an ideal Oktoberfest accompaniment, and Root Beer Jerky (page 137), of course, knows no season.

Flavored Salts

Growing up, I thought there was only one kind of salt. It came in a navy blue canister with a picture of a girl carrying an umbrella on it and the slogan, "When it rains, it pours." The salt was very fine, like sugar or sand, and tasted sharp, metallic, and a little bit tangy. I sprinkled it on soft-boiled eggs at breakfast, French fries at McDonald's, and—when my mother wasn't home to see—the mayonnaise-and-white-bread sandwiches my father and I loved to eat together.

It wasn't until my early twenties that I discovered there was a whole world of salts beyond Morton's fine-grain table salt. Coarse kosher salt was a revelation. I began keeping it in a ramekin perched next to the stove, and never went back to table salt again. Next I discovered sea salts like Maldon and fleur

de sel, which elevated many of my favorite brownie and cookie recipes to new heights. Finally, I was exposed to gourmet salts when I ate at Eden, a five-star restaurant in Banff, Alberta, Canada. There was no salt on the table, and when I asked for it, the waiter returned with a wooden box filled with different varieties, including Himalayan pink rock salt, smoked salt, and black salt.

These flavored salts are all incredibly easy to make, and they look gorgeous in their jars. The uses for them are endless. I love to use the Lemon Salt with Fennel and Red Pepper Flakes (page 116) to season chicken breasts or pork chops, the Lavender Salt (page 117) is divine sprinkled on shortbread cookies, and the Margarita Salt (page 118) is great for (what else?) rimming cocktail glasses.

Lemon Salt with Fennel and Red Pepper Flakes

Makes 1 cup, or 2 (4-ounce) jars

¹/₄ cup freshly grated lemon zest (about 3 large lemons)

¹/₄ cup coarse kosher salt

¹/₄ cup flaky sea salt, such as fleur de sel

1 tablespoon plus 1 teaspoon fennel seeds, lightly crushed with a knife

2 teaspoons red pepper flakes

Preheat the oven to 300°F. Spread the lemon zest on a baking sheet. Bake for 5 minutes. Stir the zest and continue to bake until it is dry to the touch, about 5 minutes more. Remove the baking sheet from the oven and allow the zest to cool completely, about 20 minutes.

In a medium bowl, combine the kosher salt, flaky sea salt, fennel seeds, and red pepper flakes. Add the lemon zest and stir until evenly distributed. Divide the salt mixture between 2 (4-ounce) jars with tight-fitting lids. Store in a cool, dry place for up to 6 months.

Lavender Salt

**Makes 1 cup, or
2 (4-ounce) jars**

$1/2$ **cup coarse kosher salt**

$1/2$ **cup flaky sea salt, such as fleur
de sel**

2 tablespoons dried lavender buds

Combine the kosher salt, flaky sea
salt, and lavender buds in a medium
bowl and stir to combine. Divide the
salt mixture between 2 (4-ounce) jars
with tight-fitting lids. Store in a cool,
dry place for up to a year.

Margarita Salt

**Makes 1 cup, or
2 (4-ounce) jars**

2 tablespoons freshly grated
    lime zest (about 3 medium
    limes)

2 tablespoons freshly grated
    orange zest (about 1
    medium orange)

$^1/_2$ cup coarse kosher salt

$^1/_2$ cup sugar

Preheat the oven to 300°F. Combine the lime zest and orange zest on a baking sheet. Bake for 5 minutes. Stir the zest and continue to bake until it is dry to the touch, about 5 minutes more. Remove the baking sheet from the oven and allow the zest to cool completely, about 20 minutes.

In a medium bowl, combine the salt and sugar. Add the zests and stir until evenly distributed. Divide the salt mixture between 2 (4-ounce) jars with tight-fitting lids. Store in a cool, dry place for up to 6 months.

Habanero Hot Sauce

I think hot sauce is an addictive substance. I know people who sprinkle it on scrambled eggs, add it to spaghetti sauce, and use it as a dip for pizza crust. However you choose to use it, this habanero hot sauce is especially delicious. The secret is to sauté the onion and garlic in a little bit of olive oil. It gives the finished sauce a slightly sweet, caramelized flavor. I adapted this recipe from a restaurant called Ortine in Brooklyn. They place little ramekins of the most delicious hot sauce on every table, along with the salt and pepper shakers.

MAKES ABOUT 2 CUPS, OR 2 HALF-PINT JARS

2 tablespoons olive oil

$^1/_2$ small onion, diced

3 garlic cloves, minced

1 cup stemmed, seeded, and coarsely chopped habaneros

3 cups stemmed, seeded, and coarsely chopped jalapeños

$^1/_2$ cup white vinegar

$^1/_2$ teaspoon salt

Heat the olive oil in a large heavy-bottomed pot. Add the onion and garlic and sauté, stirring frequently, until fragrant, 2 or 3 minutes. Be careful not to brown the garlic. Add the habaneros, jalapeños, vinegar, salt, and $^1/_2$ cup of water and bring it to a boil. Reduce the heat and simmer until the peppers are soft, about 20 minutes.

Transfer the pepper mixture to a blender or food processor and purée until smooth. Transfer the hot sauce to 2 clean half-pint jars and store in the refrigerator for up to a month.

Ginger Sriracha

I have some friends who are chili sauce addicts. I've seen them add sriracha to scrambled eggs, Cesar salads, grilled cheese sandwiches . . . you name it, they think it tastes better with a serious dose of garlicy hot sauce. While the bottle looks mysterious and exotic with all its Thai writing, it turns out that homemade sriracha couldn't be easier to make. I've added some freshly grated ginger to this version. Red fresno chiles have a similar heat and flavor profile to jalapeños. If you can't find red fresnos, you can substitute jalapeños in a pinch, but your sauce won't have that signature fiery color. I like to mix this sauce with a little bit of mayonnaise and spread it on turkey sandwiches.

Makes 1½ cups, or 3 (4-ounce) jars

- ½ **pound fresh red fresno chiles**
- 3 **large garlic cloves, minced**
- 1 **tablespoon freshly grated ginger**
- 2 **tablespoons sugar**
- 2 **teaspoons kosher salt**
- ¾ **cup rice wine vinegar**

Remove the stems and coarsely chop the chiles. Transfer them to a heavy-bottomed pot and add the garlic, ginger, sugar, salt, and vinegar. Bring the mixture to a boil over high heat, then reduce the heat and simmer for 5 minutes. Remove the pot from the heat and allow the mixture to cool slightly.

Transfer the mixture to a food processor or blender and blend until smooth. If it looks too thick, add a little water.

Transfer the sriracha to 6 clean (4-ounce) jars and store in the refrigerator for up to a month.

Chipotle Ketchup

One of my favorite pieces of food writing is Malcolm Gladwell's essay "The Ketchup Conundrum," which was published in the *New Yorker* in 2004. If you haven't read it, I highly recommend you look it up. Who knew America's most ubiquitous condiment could be so fascinating? In the essay Gladwell argues that people always want ketchup to taste the same, unlike mustard, which comes in a variety of flavors (Dijon, honey, spicy, etc.). I agree to a point. While I would never dispute the merits of Heinz 57, I think there is room for a bit of variation—like this chipotle ketchup with hints of cinnamon and cayenne. I adapted this recipe from several I researched in *Saveur* magazine, and on the Homesick Texan blog, and on the website Serious Eats.

MAKES ABOUT 3 CUPS OR 3 HALF-PINT JARS

1 (28-ounce) can tomato purée, preferably San Marzano

1 medium yellow onion, diced

7 tablespoons packed dark brown sugar

$^1/_2$ cup red wine vinegar

$^1/_4$ cup chopped canned chipotle chilies in adobo sauce

1 teaspoon kosher salt

1 teaspoon ground mustard

$^1/_2$ teaspoon allspice

$^1/_2$ teaspoon celery seeds

$^1/_4$ teaspoon cinnamon

$^1/_4$ teaspoon cayenne pepper

Combine the tomato purée, onion, brown sugar, vinegar, chipotle chiles, salt, ground mustard, allspice, celery seeds, cinnamon, and cayenne in a large, heavy-bottomed pot. Bring it to a boil over medium-high heat, stirring frequently. Reduce the heat and simmer until the mixture is thick and is the consistency of ketchup, about 1 hour.

Working in batches, purée the ketchup in a blender (or use an immersion blender). Return the puréed ketchup to the pot and bring it to a simmer.

Ladle the hot ketchup into 3 hot sterilized half-pint jars, leaving $^1/_4$-inch headspace. To preserve the ketchup, process the jars in a hot water bath for 15 minutes. Otherwise, store the jars in the refrigerator for up to 2 months.

Spicy Gift Packaging

You can find mason jars in a variety of sizes as most hardware stores. My favorites are the pretty diamond-quilted ones. Smaller, 4-ounce jars are great for gifts like flavored salts and homemade mustard or hot sauce. I use the standard 8-ounce (half-pint) size for things like ketchup, salsa, and relish. Larger, pint jars are perfect for pickles—because you can never have too many.

Vintage bottles and jars are also a great way to package homemade sauces and condiments. I love to shop at thrift stores and consignment shops. You never know what unique treasures you might find. Just be sure to wash them well before filling them. Stores like Pier 1 Imports, the Container Store, and Sur la Table also stock decorative and colorful glass bottles and containers.

I like to use simple nametags and gift cards for labels, but get creative with stamps, old photographs, stickers, and glittery pens.

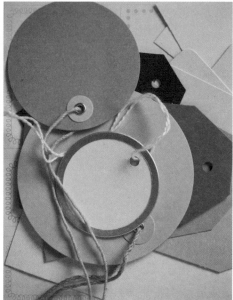

Honey-Beer Mustard

One peek inside my fridge and you can tell that I love mustard. The shelves are filled with fancy little jars of whole grain, deli style, and spicy brown. But making homemade mustard is so easy you may never be able to justify buying it again. For this recipe, I like to use a malty, dark beer, but you could substitute white wine or hard cider. You can also substitute maple syrup for the honey. This mustard is delicious on pastrami sandwiches or used as a dip for pretzels. I like to divide the mustard between six small, four-ounce canning jars to give as gifts.

MAKES ABOUT 3 CUPS, OR 6 (4-OUNCE) JARS

1 1/2 cups dark beer

1 cup mustard seeds

1 cup apple cider vinegar

1/2 cup honey

1/2 teaspoon salt

1/4 teaspoon allspice

Combine the beer and mustard seeds in a medium pot. Bring it to a boil over medium-high heat. Remove the pot from the heat and allow the mixture to stand until the mustard seeds have absorbed almost all of the liquid, 2 or 3 hours.

Transfer the mustard seeds and any remaining liquid to a food processor. Add the vinegar, honey, salt, and allspice and pulse until the seeds are coarsely ground. You may have to stop once or twice to scrape down the sides of the processor with a spatula.

Transfer the mustard to clean jars and store in the refrigerator for up to 6 months.

Chocolate Barbecue Sauce

This barbecue sauce is as dark and silky as chocolate syrup, but if you look closely you can see all the fiery flecks of chiles. The coffee really brings out the rich chocolate flavor. Because pork and chocolate are a classic Mexican combination, I like to slather this sauce over ribs, but it would also be delicious with chicken. I like spice, so I add a teaspoon of cayenne pepper to really kick things up. For a milder sauce you can certainly omit it.

Makes about 8 cups, or 8 half-pint jars

3 cups ketchup

2 cups lightly packed dark brown sugar

1 1/2 cups strong brewed coffee

3/4 cup apple cider vinegar

5 or 6 plump garlic cloves, minced (about 1/4 cup)

3 tablespoons Worcestershire sauce

3 tablespoons ancho chili powder

1 teaspoon cayenne pepper (optional)

2 ounces unsweetened chocolate, chopped (about 1/3 cup)

Combine the ketchup, brown sugar, coffee, apple cider vinegar, garlic, Worcestershire sauce, chili powder, and cayenne (if using) in a large, heavy-bottomed saucepan. Bring it to a boil over medium-high heat, stirring frequently. Stir in the chocolate. Reduce the heat to low and simmer gently until the sauce has thickened and the flavors are blended, 25 to 30 minutes. Allow the sauce to cool completely, then transfer it to airtight containers. Store it in the refrigerator for up to 2 weeks.

Balsamic-Raisin Steak Sauce

Meat lovers are divided on the subject of steak sauce. Some would argue that it's sacrilege—a good porterhouse needs no adornment. Others claim its zippy taste enhances the flavor of steak in the same way that ketchup enhances a burger. Whatever side you are on, one thing is for sure: homemade steak sauce is way better than supermarket versions. The two secret ingredients in this recipe (balsamic vinegar and raisins) add an earthy sweetness. Soy sauce and Worcestershire sauce impart that elusive, savory umami flavor. I love to bring jars of this steak sauce to summertime pool parties and barbecues. It also makes an ideal Father's Day gift. The best part? It will keep for almost the whole summer in the fridge.

Makes about 2 cups, or 2 half-pint jars

1 cup ketchup

1 large shallot, minced (about ¹/₂ cup)

¹/₄ cup Worcestershire sauce

¹/₂ cup balsamic vinegar

¹/₃ cup raisins

3 tablespoons soy sauce

2 tablespoons packed brown sugar

1 tablespoon dry mustard

Combine the ketchup, shallot, Worcestershire sauce, balsamic vinegar, raisins, soy sauce, brown sugar, and mustard in a medium saucepan. Bring it to a boil, then reduce the heat and simmer until the mixture has thickened, about 30 minutes. Using an immersion blender, purée the sauce until smooth. (Alternatively, purée the sauce in a blender.)

Transfer the sauce to 2 clean half-pint jars. The sauce will keep in the refrigerator for up to 2 months.

Spicy Tomato Confit

These oven-dried tomatoes are a great project for a lazy, summer Sunday afternoon, but you can also make them in the dead of winter with not-so-great tomatoes from the supermarket. Slow-roasting them for hours really concentrates their flavors and coaxes out their natural sweetness. The uses for these tomatoes are endless: add them to pasta dishes, salads, or soups, or use them as a pizza topping. Don't toss out the olive oil in the jars once you have used up all the tomatoes. It's incredibly flavorful. Use it to make a vinaigrette or as a dip for bread.

MAKES ABOUT 4 CUPS OR 4 HALF-PINT JARS

6 pounds plum tomatoes

1/4 cup extra-virgin olive oil, plus more for storing

2 teaspoons sugar

1/2 teaspoon red pepper flakes

Kosher salt and freshly ground pepper

4 sprigs fresh rosemary

4 sprigs fresh thyme

12 fresh basil leaves

Preheat the oven to 250°F. Cut the tomatoes in half lengthwise and toss with 1/4 cup of olive oil. Divide the tomatoes between two rimmed baking sheets. Sprinkle them with the sugar and red pepper flakes and season them with salt and pepper. Add 2 sprigs of rosemary, 2 sprigs of thyme, and 6 basil leaves to each sheet. Roast the tomatoes until they are shrunken, shriveled, and almost dry to the touch, about 5 or 6 hours.

Remove the baking sheets from the oven and allow the tomatoes to cool completely. Discard the rosemary and thyme sprigs and basil leaves. Divide the tomatoes between 4 clean half-pint jars. Add enough olive oil to the jars to cover the tomatoes completely. Store the jars in the refrigerator for up to 2 months.

Pineapple Salsa

This bright, tropical salsa is so pretty and colorful in the jar. The combination of juicy ripe tomato and sweet pineapple is a bit unexpected, but it works wonderfully. To kick the heat up a bit, try swapping the jalapeño for a spicier habanero pepper. This salsa lasts for almost a month in the fridge, but you can also process it for longer storage. Simply sterilize the empty jars and then process the filled jars in a hot water bath for 15 minutes.

MAKES 6 CUPS, or 6 HALF-PINT JArs

- 3 large tomatoes, chopped (about 3 cups)

- 1 medium pineapple, chopped (about 3 cups)

- 1 red or green bell pepper, cored, seeded, and finely chopped (about $1/2$ cup)

- 2 large jalapeño peppers, seeded and finely chopped (about $1/3$ cup)

- 1 garlic clove, minced (about 1 teaspoon)

- $3/4$ cup lemon juice

- $3/4$ cup lime juice

- 3 tablespoons chopped fresh cilantro

- 2 tablespoons honey

Combine the tomatoes, pineapple, bell pepper, jalapeño peppers, garlic, lemon juice, lime juice, cilantro, and honey in a large, heavy-bottomed pot. Bring the mixture to a boil over medium-high heat, stirring frequently. Lower the heat and simmer until the mixture thickens and some of the liquid has evaporated, about 10 to 15 minutes.

Ladle the hot salsa into 6 hot, clean half-pint jars. Store the jars in the refrigerator for up to 3 weeks.

Spicy Marinated Artichoke Hearts

In her cookbook, *Salad as a Meal*, Patricia Wells includes a wonderful recipe for marinated artichokes. What I love best about it is that it uses frozen artichoke hearts in place of fresh—you get to skip all that blanching and chopping! I've very loosely adapted her recipe here. I include lemon, thyme, and hot pepper flakes for kick. These artichoke hearts are great on their own, but I think they are especially delicious tucked into omelets or used as a topping for pizza.

Makes about 4 cups, or 4 half-pint jars

2 (9-ounce) packages frozen artichoke hearts (about 4 cups)

1 to 2 cups extra-virgin olive oil

4 fresh or dried bay leaves

4 sprigs fresh thyme

$^3/_4$ teaspoon hot pepper flakes

$^1/_2$ teaspoon salt

Zest of 1 fresh lemon, cut into thick strips

In a large saucepan, combine the artichoke hearts, 1 cup of olive oil, bay leaves, thyme, hot pepper flakes, salt, and lemon zest. Bring to a simmer and cook over low heat until the artichoke hearts are heated through, about 10 minutes. Remove the pan from the heat and allow the mixture to cool completely.

Divide the artichokes, bay leaves, and thyme sprigs evenly between 4 clean half-pint jars. Pour the olive oil over the artichokes covering them completely (you may need to add more olive oil). The artichokes will keep for up to 2 months in the refrigerator.

Bread-and-Butter Zucchini Relish

I used to be a bit of a purist when it came to hot dogs. Nothing but mustard for me, thanks! But then I learned how to make this relish. Zucchini replaces cucumber for an unexpected twist. It's sweet like bread-and-butter pickles, but not fake-tasting, like some store-bought relishes can be. Bring a jar or two along to your next cookout.

MAKES ABOUT 6 CUPS, OR 6 HALF-PINT JARS

3 medium zucchini, finely chopped (about 4 cups)

2 red bell peppers, finely chopped (about 2 cups)

1 medium yellow onion, finely chopped (about 1 cup)

$^1/_4$ cup kosher salt

1 $^1/_2$ cups sugar

3 cups white vinegar

1 tablespoon mustard seeds

1 tablespoon celery seeds

$^1/_4$ teaspoon turmeric

Combine the zucchini, red bell pepper, and onion in a large bowl. Sprinkle with the salt, cover with cold water, and soak the vegetables for 2 hours. Drain and rinse the vegetables.

In a large pot, combine the sugar, vinegar, mustard seeds, celery seeds, and turmeric. Bring it to a boil and cook, stirring until the sugar dissolves. Add the vegetable mixture and return to a boil. Cook until the vegetables are heated through, about 10 minutes.

Ladle the hot relish into 6 clean half-pint jars. Store the relish in the refrigerator for up to 3 weeks. For longer storage, process the jars in a hot water bath for 10 minutes. Processed relish will keep for a year, stored in a cool, dry place.

Blue Cheese and Almond-Stuffed Olives

These nutty, cheesy olives are a delicious one-bite snack on their own, but they also make a fantastic addition to a martini. To give them as gifts, wash the olive jars in hot, soapy water to remove the labels. Then when you re-jar the olives, tie a card around the top with your favorite dirty martini recipe.

Makes about 4 cups, or 2 (10-ounce) jars

- $1/4$ cup whole almonds, toasted and cooled
- $1/2$ cup blue cheese, room temperature
- 2 (10-ounce) jars large pitted green olives, about 3 cups

Place the almonds in the work bowl of a food processor and pulse them until they're coarsely ground. Add the blue cheese and pulse it until combined. Transfer the mixture to a bowl.

Drain the olives into a bowl, reserving the brine. Fill the olives with the blue cheese mixture (about $1/2$ teaspoon per olive). Return the olives to the jars and top with the reserved brine. The olives will keep in the refrigerator for up to a month.

Pickled Fennel

Crunchy, anise-flavored fennel pairs especially well with sweet, juicy orange. I love to serve slices of pickled fennel alongside sandwiches as an alternative to traditional cucumber pickles. Pickled fennel is also delicious tossed into salads, layered on bruschetta spread with goat cheese, or used as a garnish for Bloody Marys. Fennel seeds are a nice addition to this recipe, but if you don't have any on hand you can leave them out. Don't slice the fennel too thinly; you want it to retain some crunch. Aim for $1/4$-inch-thick strips.

Makes about 4 cups, or 2 pint jars

2 medium bulbs fennel (about 1 $1/2$ to 2 pounds total)

2 oranges, zest removed in strips

3 cups white vinegar

1 cup sugar

1 tablespoon fennel seeds (optional)

2 teaspoons kosher salt

2 sprigs fresh thyme

Cut each fennel bulb in half vertically. Slice out the core. Slice the fennel into $1/4$-inch-thick strips. Set aside.

Juice the oranges. Combine the orange juice, zest, vinegar, sugar, fennel seeds (if using), and salt in a large pot. Add 1 cup of water and bring it to a boil, stirring to dissolve the sugar. Add the fennel slices and thyme sprigs and simmer until the fennel is very slightly wilted, about 5 minutes.

Divide the fennel and pickling liquid between 4 clean half-pint jars. Allow the fennel to marinate in the refrigerator for 2 days. Pickled fennel will keep in the refrigerator for up to 3 weeks. But you can also process the jars in a hot water bath for longer storage. The processed jars will keep for up to a year stored in a cool, dark place.

Root Beer Jerky

For a long time, I thought I didn't like jerky. That's because the only jerky I'd ever tasted was the kind sold by the cash register at gas stations. Real, homemade jerky is intensely chewy, peppery, and beefy. It's easy to make, and the variations are endless. I love the slightly sweet, sarsaparilla flavor the root beer adds to this recipe, but you could substitute Coke, Dr Pepper, or beer. Ask your butcher to slice the meat for you—it saves a lot of work! If you are going to slice it yourself, freeze the meat for an hour first—it makes the work much easier. To give this as a gift, put small bags of jerky in pint glasses and tie with a ribbon.

MAKES ABOUT ³/₄ POUND

1 cup root beer

¹/₂ cup soy sauce

¹/₄ cup red wine vinegar

2 tablespoons packed dark brown sugar

1 teaspoon freshly ground black pepper

¹/₂ teaspoon red pepper flakes

2 pounds very lean top sirloin or flank steak, sliced against the grain into ¹/₄-inch thick strips

Vegetable oil for oiling the wire racks

Combine the root beer, soy sauce, vinegar, and brown sugar in a medium saucepan and bring it to a boil. Reduce the heat and simmer until the mixture is reduced to 1 cup, about 15 minutes. Remove from the heat and let it cool completely. Stir in the pepper and red pepper flakes.

Put the sliced steak in a large, zip-topped plastic bag and pour the marinade over the steak. Seal the bag and refrigerate overnight.

Preheat the oven to 200°F and position the racks in the middle and lower positions. Line 2 large baking sheets with foil and place a large wire rack on each. Lightly oil the racks with the vegetable oil.

Remove the beef from the marinade and pat it dry with paper towels. (Discard the extra marinade.) Arrange the beef slices on the racks, leaving a little space between each one. Bake until the jerky is firm and dry but still bendable, about 3 to 4 hours.

Allow the jerky to cool completely. Store it in a plastic bag in the refrigerator for up to 6 weeks.

Dill-Pickled Brussels Sprouts

I usually prepare Brussels sprouts by roasting them with plenty of olive oil, salt, pepper, and a drizzle of maple syrup until they are caramelized and golden-brown. But Brussels sprouts also make delicious crunchy, briny pickles. I like to flavor mine with garlic, dill, and red pepper flakes for kick, but feel free to play around with the spices. Peppercorns, fresh fennel fronds, mustard seeds, and whole dried chiles would also be great additions. You can preserve these sprouts for longer storage by sterilizing the empty jars and processing the filled and sealed jars in a hot water bath for 10 minutes. They will keep for a year on the shelf. A jar of pickled Brussels sprouts makes a wonderful fall hostess gift. I like to serve them as part of an antipasti platter with lots of different cheeses and charcuterie.

Makes 6 Pints

- 3 tablespoons sea salt, plus more

- 2 pounds small Brussels sprouts (about 8 cups)

- 1 medium red onion, thinly sliced (about 1 cup)

- 6 whole garlic cloves, peeled

- 6 tablespoons coarsely chopped fresh dill

- 1 1/2 teaspoons red pepper flakes (optional)

- 3 cups cider vinegar

- 2 tablespoons sugar

Fill a large bowl with ice water. Bring a large pot of salted water to a boil. Add the Brussels sprouts and cook them until they are bright green, about 2 or 3 minutes. Drain the Brussels sprouts and immediately submerge them in ice water.

Drain the cooled Brussels sprouts and divide them evenly between 6 clean pint jars. Divide the red onion evenly between the jars. Add 1 clove of garlic and 1 tablespoon of dill to each jar. Add 1/4 teaspoon red pepper flakes to each jar, if using.

Combine the vinegar, 3 tablespoons of salt, the sugar, and 3 cups of water in a medium saucepan. Bring it to a boil over medium heat, stirring until the salt and sugar are dissolved. Carefully pour the hot brine over the Brussels sprouts, covering them completely.

Allow the jars to cool, then seal them and store in the refrigerator for up to a month.

Apple Cider Jelly

Slow Cooker Caramel Apple Butter

Berry Lemon Curd

Carrot Cake Conserve

Honey-Ginger Pumpkin Butter

Vanilla-Orange Marmalade

Blueberry-Port Jam

Plum Conserve

Strawberry-Balsamic-Thyme Jam

Peach Jam with Lavender and Honey

Rosemary-Pear Jam

Cherry-Apricot Chutney

Concord Grape Jam

Cranberry-Champagne Jam with Crystallized Ginger

Bourbon-Bacon Jam

Winter Fig Jam

Fig and Onion Marmalade

I'm a little bit of a jam fanatic. I make a batch almost every week, inspired by whatever fruit is in season. Of course I can't use it all myself (no one eats that much toast!), so I often end up giving it away. My friends and family have come to expect a jar of my latest creation every time they see me, and I rarely disappoint. Jam just might be the perfect food gift: it's sweet, pretty, and delicious, and it is also incredibly portable.

I've made an effort to include diverse recipes in this chapter that use fruit from all seasons. You don't have to stop canning just because strawberries are no longer available. You can make delicious preserves with cranberries, apples, and oranges. Many of these recipes are for sweet preserves, but there are some savories as well, such as Fig and Onion Marmalade (page 168) and Bourbon-Bacon Jam (page 166). Most of the recipes call for adding ¼ to ½ teaspoon of butter to the pot with the preserves. It might seem like an odd ingredient, but the butter helps to reduce foaming.

Making jams, jellies, and other preserves is a relatively simple process. Generally speaking, preserves will keep well in the refrigerator for several months. You can also process the jars for longer storage. First prepare the jars and lids: place the jars on a rack in a large pot. Add enough water to cover the jars completely. Bring the pot to a boil over high heat. Turn off

the heat and allow the jars to rest in the hot water. Meanwhile, put the bands and lids in a small saucepan and cover them with water. Heat over medium heat until the water is simmering, then remove the pan from the heat and allow the bands and lids to rest in the hot water.

To fill the jars, ladle the hot preserves into the jars, leaving a quarter inch of headspace. Place a lid on each jar and screw the bands on until they are just barely tight. Place the jars on a rack in a pot and cover them completely with water. Cover the pot and bring it to a boil over high heat. Boil for ten to fifteen minutes. Turn off the heat, uncover the pot, and allow the jars to rest in the water for five minutes. Remove the jars from the pot and allow them to rest undisturbed on a countertop for six hours or overnight. Check the seals; they should be indented.

Many, but not all, of these recipes call for added pectin. Pectin is a natural thickener found in fruits. It is what causes preserves to thicken and gel. You can certainly make preserves without it, but you need to add a lot of sugar and cook it for a much longer period of time. I always use one of two kinds of pectin: regular powdered fruit pectin, which can be found in many supermarkets, for traditional sweet jams and jellies, and Pomona's Universal Pectin, which is great for making low- or no-sugar preserves. Pomona's Universal Pectin can be found in some well-stocked supermarkets, and at pomonapectin.com.

Apple Cider Jelly

Making jelly can be a complicated, multistep procedure. Usually, you must first extract the juice from the fruit by boiling it down and filtering it through a special jelly bag. But by using fresh apple cider you can skip all of that. Instead, it's a simple process of simmering the cider with sugar and spices. This jelly has an intense, tangy apple flavor that is complimented by a luxurious, molasses-y note from the brown sugar. It would be a delicious accompaniment to buttery breads like challah or brioche, or try it with ginger or pumpkin bread.

MAKES ABOUT 6 CUPS, OR 6 HALF-PINT JARS

5 cups apple cider

1 cup packed dark brown sugar

1 cinnamon stick

1 strip lemon or orange zest

1/2 teaspoon whole cloves

1 (1.75-ounce) package regular
    powdered fruit pectin

3 cups sugar

Combine the apple cider and brown sugar in a large, heavy-bottomed pot. Tie the cinnamon stick, lemon zest, and cloves in a piece of cheesecloth and add it to the pot. Sprinkle the pectin evenly over the cider and whisk to blend. Bring the mixture to a boil over high heat, stirring frequently. Add the sugar all at once and return the mixture to a full rolling boil, stirring constantly. Boil hard for 1 minute.

Remove the pot from the heat and discard the cheesecloth. Skim any foam from the surface of the jelly with a cold metal spoon. Ladle the hot jelly into 6 hot, clean half-pint jars. To preserve the jelly, process the jars in a hot water bath for 10 minutes. The preserved jelly will keep for up to a year on the shelf. Otherwise, store the jars in the refrigerator for up to 2 months.

best wishes

Slow Cooker Caramel Apple Butter

It's time to dust off that old-fashioned crock pot! Using a slow cooker makes preparing this apple butter a breeze. I like to use a mixture of tart granny smith and sweet honey crisp apples. I adapted this recipe from an article I read by Marisa McClellan, author of *Food in Jars*. If you don't have a slow cooker, don't despair. You can simmer the puréed applesauce in a pot on the stove over very low heat, stirring frequently, for about three hours.

MAKES ABOUT 7 CUPS, OR 7 HALF-PINT JARS

6 pounds apples, peeled, cored, and cut into 1-inch chunks

²/₃ cup apple cider, apple juice, or water

2 cups packed dark brown sugar

2 teaspoons cinnamon

¹/₂ teaspoon ground ginger

¹/₂ teaspoon nutmeg

Combine the apples and apple cider, juice, or water in a large, heavy-bottomed pot. Bring it to a boil, then reduce the heat and simmer until the apples are soft enough to break apart with a spoon, about 30 minutes. Remove the pot from the heat and purée the apples with an immersion blender. (Alternatively, this can be done in batches in a blender or food processor.)

Transfer the applesauce to a slow cooker and stir in the brown sugar, cinnamon, ginger, and nutmeg. Cook on low for 8 hours, until the butter is thick enough to hold its shape when spooned on a chilled plate.

Ladle the hot apple butter into 7 hot, clean half-pint jars. To preserve the butter, process the jars in a hot water bath for 10 minutes. Preserved apple butter will keep on the shelf for up to a year. Otherwise, store the jars in the refrigerator for up to 2 months.

Berry Lemon Curd

Spread on toast, biscuits, or English muffins, tart and silky lemon curd is a decadent alternative to jam. It also makes a terrific dessert spooned into a pastry shell or sandwiched between shortbread cookies. Incorporating puréed berries into this curd gives it a pretty pink hue and just a touch of berry sweetness.

Makes about 1 1/2 cups, or three 4-ounce jars

- 1/4 **pound (1 stick) unsalted butter, room temperature**
- **1 cup sugar**
- **Freshly grated zest from 3 lemons**
- 1/2 **cup lemon juice (3 to 4 lemons)**
- 1/4 **cup raspberries, blackberries, or sliced fresh strawberries**
- **5 large egg yolks**

In a large bowl, beat the butter, sugar, and lemon zest with an electric mixer until well combined.

Combine the lemon juice and berries in a blender and blend until smooth. Add the lemon juice mixture to the sugar mixture and beat until just combined. Beat in the egg yolks one at a time.

Transfer the mixture to a medium-sized, heavy-bottomed pot. Cook the mixture over low heat, stirring constantly, until it is thick and creamy, about 12 minutes. It will register 170°F on a candy thermometer.

Immediately strain the curd through a fine mesh sieve into a bowl. Ladle the curd into jars, cool to room temperature, then seal the jars and store them in the refrigerator for up to 2 weeks. For longer storage, process the jars in a hot water bath for 15 minutes. The processed lemon curd will keep for 3 months stored in a cool, dry place.

Carrot Cake Conserve

This carrot cake conserve is just the thing to make in March or early April, when you are itching for spring to arrive. Loaded with raisins, walnuts, and juicy chunks of pineapple, it tastes exactly like carrot cake. Needless to say, this conserve is especially delicious when paired with cream cheese. The inspiration for this jam came from a recipe from the *Ball Complete Book of Home Preserving*.

Makes 6 cups, or 6 half-pint jars

3 cups granulated sugar

3 teaspoons Pomona's Universal pectin

1/2 cup raisins

1 1/2 cups finely grated peeled carrots

1 1/2 cups finely diced peeled and cored tart apples, such as granny smith

1 3/4 cups canned crushed pineapple, including juice

3 tablespoons freshly squeezed lemon juice

3/4 teaspoon cinnamon

4 teaspoons calcium water (included in the Pomona's box)

1/4 teaspoon butter

1/2 cup finely chopped walnuts

Combine the sugar and pectin in a medium bowl and whisk to blend. Pulse the raisins in a food processor until they are finely chopped.

Combine the carrots, apples, pineapple, lemon juice, cinnamon, and calcium water in a large, heavy saucepan. Bring to a boil, stirring constantly. Reduce the heat to a simmer, cover, and cook, stirring occasionally, until the apples have softened, about 20 minutes.

Stir in the raisins. Add the sugar-pectin mixture and the butter and return the mixture to a full rolling boil. Boil hard for 1 minute. Stir in the walnuts.

Remove the pot from the heat and skim any foam from the surface of the conserve. Ladle the hot conserve into 6 hot, clean half-pint jars. To preserve the conserve, process it in a hot water bath for 10 minutes. The preserved conserve will keep for up to a year on the shelf. Otherwise, store the jars in the refrigerator for up to 2 months.

Honey-Ginger Pumpkin Butter

Standard recipes for pumpkin butter invariably call for loads of brown sugar and cinnamon, and the results taste almost exactly like pumpkin pie filling. It's always delicious, but it's not exactly novel. For this recipe, I decided to change things up by incorporating honey, apple, and freshly grated ginger. The resulting pumpkin butter is lighter in flavor than traditional versions, with a delicate sweetness and pronounced zing. The grated apple lends a juicy, fruity note, while spices like cinnamon, nutmeg, and cloves add warmth and a hint of familiarity.

MAKES ABOUT 3 CUPS, OR 3 HALF-PINT JARS

1 (15-ounce) can solid, packed pumpkin

$^3/_4$ cup apple cider

1 large apple, peeled and grated

$^1/_2$ cup honey

2 heaping tablespoons freshly grated ginger

$^1/_2$ teaspoon cinnamon

$^1/_4$ teaspoon ground ginger

$^1/_4$ teaspoon nutmeg

Pinch of cloves

Combine the pumpkin, apple cider, grated apple, honey, fresh ginger, cinnamon, ground ginger, nutmeg, and cloves in a heavy-bottomed, medium saucepan. Bring it to a boil over medium-high heat, stirring frequently. Reduce the heat and simmer until the mixture is thick, about 1 hour. Divide the pumpkin butter between 3 clean half-pint jars and store them in the refrigerator for up to 2 months.

Vanilla-Orange Marmalade

Homemade orange marmalade is bright, sweet, and bursting with fresh citrus flavor, and the vanilla bean infuses it with spicy warmth. I use two kinds of oranges because the juice is better from the juice oranges, but the zest is better from the navels. This recipe is a bit time-consuming and requires a lot of chopping (some of which can be done in the food processor) but trust me—the results are absolutely worth it. This marmalade is so delicious I promise you will leap out of bed in the morning excited for breakfast. You will also find yourself dreaming up new ways to eat it: swirled into yogurt, spooned over ice cream, and sandwiched between shortbread cookies. I loosely adapted this recipe from a publication from the University of California Davis's Division of Agriculture and Natural Resources.

MAKES ABOUT 8 CUPS OR 8 HALF-PINT JARS

6 $^1/_2$ cups sugar

2 medium juice oranges

2 large navel oranges

2 lemons

2 $^1/_2$ cups water

$^1/_8$ teaspoon baking soda

1 vanilla bean

1 (1.75-ounce) package regular fruit pectin

$^1/_4$ teaspoon butter

Measure 6 $^1/_2$ cups of sugar into a large bowl and set aside.

Wash the oranges and lemons. Remove the rinds in quarters and thinly slice them lengthwise. When all the rinds are sliced, roughly chop them crosswise into slightly smaller pieces. Put the rinds in a large pot and add the water and the baking soda.

With a sharp knife, split the vanilla bean open lengthwise and scrape the seeds into the pot. Add the vanilla bean to the pot and bring it to a boil. Reduce the heat, cover, and simmer for 15 minutes.

Meanwhile, roughly chop the oranges and lemons and remove the seeds. Transfer the fruit to a food processor and pulse until it is evenly chopped but still a bit coarse. Add the fruit to the pot with the rinds and return it to a boil. Cover and boil for 15 minutes.

Measure out 4 $^1/_2$ cups of the fruit mixture. Make sure to get a good mixture of rind, fruit, and juice. Discard the remaining fruit mixture and vanilla bean. Return the reserved 4 $^1/_2$ cups of fruit mixture to the pot. Stir in the pectin and the butter and return it to a boil. Boil vigorously for 1 minute.

Add the sugar all at once and stir until combined. Return it to a rapid boil, stirring frequently, and boil hard for 1 minute. Remove the pot from the heat and skim any foam from the surface of the jam. Ladle the jam into 8 hot, clean half-pint jars. To preserve the jam, process the jars in a hot water bath for 10 minutes. Otherwise, store in the refrigerator for up to 2 months.

Too Much Jam?

If you love making jam as much as I do, at some point you may find yourself with a surplus of jars. Since there are only so many peanut butter and jam sandwiches a person can eat, here are some creative and delicious uses for extra jam.

- Swirl it into pound cake, banana bread, or brownie batter.

- Use it to sandwich gingersnaps, shortbread, or peanut butter cookies.

- Warm jam in a saucepan over low heat just until it softens. Pour the warm jam over ice cream.

- Apple Cider Jelly (page 146), Rosemary-Pear Jam (page 160), and Winter Fig Jam (page 167) would all make a great glaze for roast chicken.

Blueberry-Port Jam

I was inspired to make this jam after seeing a recipe for blackberry-port jam in *Better Homes and Gardens*. I thought blueberries would be even more delicious. And what better way to enjoy port—normally thought of as a wintery drink—in the summer months? This jam has a deep, dark purple hue that looks almost black in the jar. The blueberries and port work together to create an intense, full-bodied jam bursting with ripe fruit flavors. In addition to the berries, there are notes of plum, cherry, and raisin. Try it in a peanut butter sandwich, or as a filling between two layers of lemon cake.

Makes about 7 cups, or 7 half-pint jars

5 $^1/_2$ cups sugar

3 pints fresh blueberries

1 (1.75 ounce) package regular powdered fruit pectin

1 cup ruby port

$^1/_4$ teaspoon unsalted butter

$^1/_4$ teaspoon ground cinnamon

$^1/_8$ teaspoon ground cloves

Measure 5 $^1/_2$ cups sugar into a large bowl and set aside.

Working in batches, coarsely purée the blueberries in a blender or food processor. You should have 7 cups. Transfer the blueberry purée to a large, heavy-bottomed pot. Whisk in the pectin until dissolved. Add the port, butter, cinnamon, and cloves and cook over medium-high heat, stirring constantly, until the mixture comes to a full rolling boil.

Add the sugar all at once and continue to cook, stirring constantly, until the mixture returns to a full rolling boil. Boil hard for 1 minute.

Remove the pot from the heat and skim off any foam from the surface of the jam. Ladle the hot jam into 7 hot, clean half-pint jars. To preserve the jam, process the jars in a hot water bath for 10 minutes. Preserved jam will keep for up to a year on the shelf. Otherwise, store the jam in the refrigerator for up to 2 months.

Plum Conserve

A jam with nuts in it is technically called a conserve, and they usually involve dried fruit too. This version is bursting with juicy, ripe plums, sweet golden raisins, and crunchy walnuts. Because of the play of textures and flavors, conserves are especially good over ice cream or stirred into yogurt. You can also serve them as a sweet accompaniment to grilled meats. The color of this conserve is a downright gorgeous shade of dark ruby red, and the flavor is complex and nuanced. First and foremost you get the bright, fresh plums; followed by citrusy hints of orange and lemon; and finally the spicy cinnamon and nutty walnuts. I very loosely adapted this recipe from Elise Bauer, of the fabulous website Simply Recipes.

If you aren't sure if your preserves have reached the gel stage, test it. Place a small plate in the freezer for a few minutes. Spoon a little bit of jam onto the plate and return it to the freezer for 1 minute. Take it out and drag your fingertip through the jam and tilt the plate from side to side. If the jam stays put and doesn't run, you're good to go. If not, keep simmering and testing.

MAKES ABOUT 6 CUPS, OR 6 HALF-PINT JARS

3 pounds firm-ripe plums, pitted and chopped

4 cups sugar

Zest and juice of 1 medium orange

Zest and juice of 1 lemon

1 1/2 cups golden raisins

1 cinnamon stick

1 cup chopped walnuts

Combine the plums, sugar, orange zest and juice, lemon zest and juice, raisins, and cinnamon stick in a large, heavy-bottomed pot. Bring it to a boil over medium-high heat and cook, stirring frequently, until the mixture thickens and reaches the gel stage, about 30 minutes (it will register 220°F on a candy thermometer).

Remove the pot from the heat and stir in the walnuts. Ladle the hot conserve into 6 hot, clean half-pint jars. To preserve the conserve, process the jars in a hot water bath for 10 minutes. Otherwise, store in the refrigerator for up to 2 months.

Strawberry-Balsamic-Thyme Jam

The idea for this jam came about on an early summer day just as strawberries were coming into season. I had recently invested in a bottle of expensive aged balsamic vinegar, and I was itching to use it. I also had a bunch of leftover fresh thyme in my fridge that was about to go bad. The results are insanely delicious; equal parts sweet and sophisticated. The balsamic vinegar adds depth of flavor and brings out the juicy, sunny taste of the strawberries. And the thyme, oh the thyme! It provides an addictive, lemony, herby essence that had me dreaming of slathering it over grilled bread with ricotta.

Makes 8 cups, or 8 half-pint jars

- 7 cups sugar
- 5 cups strawberries, crushed (about 8 cups of stemmed, hulled, and sliced strawberries)
- 1/4 cup best quality balsamic vinegar
- 1 tablespoon minced fresh thyme leaves
- 1 (1.75-ounce) package regular powdered fruit pectin
- 1/4 teaspoon unsalted butter

Measure 7 cups of sugar into a large bowl and set aside.

Combine the crushed strawberries, balsamic vinegar, and thyme in a large, heavy saucepan or stockpot. Whisk in the pectin until dissolved. Add the butter and bring the mixture to a full rolling boil over high heat, stirring constantly.

Add the sugar all at once and stir until it dissolves. Stirring constantly, return the mixture to a full rolling boil. Boil hard for 1 minute. Remove the pot from the heat and skim off any foam from the surface of the jam. Ladle the jam into 8 hot, clean half-pint jars. To preserve the jam, process the jars in a hot water bath for 10 minutes. Otherwise, store in the refrigerator for up to 2 months.

Peach Jam with Lavender and Honey

Do you remember when you realized lavender was delicious? I was at a farmers' market, where I bought a package of shortbread cookies speckled with the dusty purple buds. The delicate flavor and floral perfume blew me away. Where had lavender been all my culinary life? While lavender buds are edible, they often get stuck in your teeth and can be a bit tough and chewy. To impart their flavor without actually stirring them into this jam, I steeped them in a tea. When straining the tea, be sure to press down on the buds to release as much of their perfume as possible. This jam would make a lovely gift for your mother-in-law, or bridal shower favor.

MAKES ABOUT 6 CUPS OR 6 HALF-PINT JARS

2 tablespoons plus 1 teaspoon dried lavender buds, divided

1 1/2 cups honey

3 teaspoons Pomona's Universal Pectin

3 to 3 1/2 pounds of fresh, ripe peaches, pitted, peeled, and coarsely puréed (about 4 cups)*

1/4 cup freshly squeezed lemon juice (about 2 lemons)

4 teaspoons calcium water (included in the Pomona's box)

1/4 teaspoon unsalted butter

Put 2 tablespoons of the lavender buds in a small bowl and pour 1/2 cup of boiling water over them. Let them steep for 10 minutes, then strain the "tea" into a bowl and discard the buds.

Combine the honey and pectin in a medium bowl and whisk to blend.

Combine the peaches, lemon juice, rosemary, calcium water, lavender tea, and the remaining teaspoon of lavender in a large, heavy-bottomed saucepan and bring it to a boil over medium heat, stirring frequently. Add the honey-pectin mixture and the butter and return the mixture to a full rolling boil. Boil for one minute.

Remove the pot from the heat and skim any foam from the surface of the jam. Ladle the hot jam into 6 hot, clean half-pint jars. To preserve the jam, process the jars in a hot water bath for 10 minutes. The preserved jam will keep for up to a year on the shelf. Otherwise, store the jars in the refrigerator for up to 2 months.

*Note: An easy way to peel peaches is to cut a shallow 'x' in the bottom and drop them into a pot of boiling water for 20 to 30 seconds. Then plunge the peaches into ice water to cool. The skins should slip right off.

Rosemary-Pear Jam

Ripe pears are fat, juicy, and incredibly flavorful. For this recipe, I paired them (no pun intended) with fresh rosemary and just a bit of sugar. The results are fruity, herbaceous, and mildly sweet. This jam would be perfect slathered on a ham sandwich, or alongside any holiday cheese plate. Pomona's Universal Pectin is great for making low- or no-sugar jams. You can find it at well-stocked supermarkets or online at pomonapectin.com.

MAKES ABOUT 6 CUPS OR 6 HALF-PINT JARS

1 ¹/₂ cups sugar

3 teaspoons Pomona's Universal Pectin

7 or 8 medium ripe pears, cored and coarsely puréed (about 4 cups)

¹/₄ cup freshly squeezed lemon juice (about 2 lemons)

4 teaspoons calcium water (included in the Pomona's box)

2 heaping teaspoons minced fresh rosemary

¹/₄ teaspoon unsalted butter

Combine the sugar and pectin in a medium bowl and whisk to blend.

Combine the pears, lemon juice, calcium water, and rosemary in a large, heavy-bottomed saucepan and bring it to a boil over medium heat, stirring frequently. Add the sugar-pectin mixture and the butter and return the mixture to a full rolling boil. Boil for 1 minute.

Remove the pot from the heat and skim any foam from the surface of the jam. Ladle the hot jam into 6 hot, clean half-pint jars. To preserve the jam, process the jars in a hot water bath for 10 minutes. The preserved jam will keep for up to a year on the shelf. Otherwise, store the jars in the refrigerator for up to 2 months.

Cherry-Apricot Chutney

Some chutney recipes include a laundry list of spices, which can be more than a little intimidating. I've pared this fruity version down to the bare necessities. I think cherries and apricots are a great combination, and I also love the way the orange apricots look in the jar. This chutney is absolutely perfect with pork chops, but it would be delicious paired with chicken or lamb as well.

Makes about 5 cups or 5 half-pint jars

2 cups cider vinegar

$^3/_4$ cup packed brown sugar

$1^1/_2$ to 2 pounds fresh sweet cherries, pitted and chopped (about 4 cups)

1 cup chopped onion

$^3/_4$ cup chopped dried apricots

1 tablespoon mustard seeds

$^1/_2$ teaspoon salt

$^1/_2$ teaspoon allspice

1 cinnamon stick

Bring the vinegar and brown sugar to a boil in a large, heavy-bottomed pot, stirring frequently. Add the cherries, onion, apricots, mustard seeds, salt, allspice, and the cinnamon stick. Return the mixture to a boil, then reduce the heat and simmer until the mixture has thickened, about 30 minutes.

Remove the pot from the heat and ladle the hot chutney into 5 hot, clean half-pint jars. To preserve the chutney, process the jars in a hot water bath for 15 minutes. The preserved chutney will keep for up to a year on the shelf. Otherwise, store the jars in the refrigerator for up to a month.

Concord Grape Jam

There are very few foods in this world that I truly hate, but one of them is grape jelly. I think it's fake-tasting, too sweet, and lacking in any true grape flavor. I cringe when my toast comes with those little purple packets at restaurants, and I prefer my peanut butter sandwiches with strawberry jam. But guess what. Homemade concord grape jam tastes nothing like the sticky-sweet supermarket kind. It has a deep, concentrated grape flavor, and is equally tart and sweet. Adding a little bit of Pomona's Universal Pectin (pomonapectin.com) helps this jam set up quickly and keeps you from having to add a ton of sugar, but you can make it without it. Increase the sugar to six cups and simmer the jam, stirring frequently, until it reaches the jell stage, about forty-five minutes. I like to pair jars of this jam with fancy peanut butter or Pistachio-Honey Butter (page 102) for a sweet back-to-school gift. It's also delicious sandwiched between peanut butter cookies or swirled into banana bread batter.

MAKES ABOUT 6 CUPS, OR 6 HALF-PINT JARS

2 cups sugar

2 teaspoons Pomona's Universal Pectin

2 1/2 pounds concord grapes with seeds (about 8 cups)

2 teaspoons freshly squeezed lemon juice

2 teaspoons calcium water (included in the Pomona's Pectin package)

1/4 teaspoon unsalted butter

Combine the sugar and pectin in a medium bowl and whisk to blend.

Separate the grape skins from the pulp by squeezing the grapes between your fingers. Put the skins in the work bowl of a food processor and pulse until they are coarsely chopped. Transfer them to a large heavy-bottomed pot and add 1/4 cup of water. Bring to a simmer and cook until the skins have softened a bit, about 10 minutes.

Meanwhile, place the grape pulp in a medium saucepan and bring it to a boil. Reduce the heat and simmer until the grapes lose their shape, about 10 minutes. Pour the grape pulp through a fine mesh sieve into a large bowl. Force out as much pulp as you can and discard the seeds.

Add the grape pulp to the pot with the grape skins and stir to combine. Add the lemon juice and calcium water and bring it to a boil, stirring constantly. Add the sugar-pectin mixture and the butter. Bring the mixture to a full rolling boil, stirring constantly. Boil hard for 1 minute.

Remove the pot from the heat and skim any foam from the surface of the jam. Ladle the hot jam into 6 hot, clean half-pint jars. To preserve the jam, process the jars in a hot water bath for 10 minutes. The preserved jam will keep for up to a year on the shelf. Otherwise, store the jars in the refrigerator for up to 2 months.

HAPPY BIRTHDAY TO YOU!

Cranberry-Champagne Jam with Crystallized Ginger

I grew up in a house next to a cranberry bog, which is I think why I love them so much. Every fall I look forward to their arrival on supermarket shelves, and cranberry sauce has always been my favorite part of the Thanksgiving feast. The Champagne in this jam makes it especially festive, and the dried cranberries and crystallized ginger add texture, sweetness, and zing. In addition to being perfect for Thanksgiving, this jam makes a great stocking stuffer or New Year's gift.

Makes about 6 cups or 6 half-pint jars

- 1 (12-ounce) bag fresh cranberries (about 3 cups)
- 2 cups Champagne or other sparkling wine
- 1 (1.75-ounce) package regular powdered fruit pectin
- ¼ teaspoon butter
- ½ cup chopped dried cranberries
- ½ cup chopped crystallized ginger
- 4½ cups sugar

Pulse the cranberries in a food processor until they are coarsely chopped. Transfer them to a large, heavy-bottomed pot and add the Champagne. Bring them to a boil, then lower the heat and simmer until the cranberries have softened, about 10 minutes.

Sprinkle the pectin over the cranberry mixture and stir to combine. Stir in the butter. Return the mixture to a boil. Add the dried cranberries, the crystallized ginger, and then the sugar all at once. Return the mixture to a boil and boil hard for 1 minute.

Remove the pot from the heat and skim any foam from the surface of the jam. Ladle the hot jam into 6 hot, clean half-pint jars. To preserve the jam, process the jars in a hot water bath for 10 minutes. The preserved jam will keep for up to a year on the shelf. Otherwise, store it in the refrigerator for up to 2 months.

Bourbon-Bacon Jam

Sometimes a recipe can haunt you. When I first saw a recipe for bacon jam in Martha Stewart's *Everyday Food*, I thought about it for weeks. I imagined slathering it on toast, adding it to grilled cheese, spooning it over pancakes, and eating it straight from the jar. What could be more appealing than sweet, gooey jam infused with the flavors of brown sugar, maple syrup, coffee, and bacon? When I finally made it, I adapted the recipe slightly to include bourbon, which imparts a complex, oaky note. Be forewarned that this jam needs to simmer for several hours to reach a syrupy consistency. If you don't want to be relegated to your stove for that long, you can also cook it in a slow cooker, uncovered on high, for $3^{1}/_{2}$ to 4 hours.

MAKES ABOUT 3 CUPS, OR 3 HALF-PINT JARS

- 1 $^{1}/_{2}$ pounds bacon
- 2 medium onions, diced
- 3 garlic cloves, peeled and coarsely chopped
- $^{1}/_{2}$ cup cider vinegar
- $^{1}/_{2}$ cup packed dark brown sugar
- $^{1}/_{4}$ cup maple syrup
- 6 tablespoons brewed coffee
- 6 tablespoons bourbon

Divide the bacon between two large skillets and cook over medium-high heat, flipping occasionally, until the fat is rendered and the bacon is lightly browned and starting to crisp, about 10 to 15 minutes.

Transfer the bacon to paper towels to drain. Crumble it into roughly 2-inch pieces. Pour 2 tablespoons of the bacon drippings into a large, heavy-bottomed pot or Dutch oven and heat over medium-high heat. Add the onions and garlic and cook, stirring frequently, until the onions are softened and translucent, about 5 minutes. Add the vinegar, brown sugar, maple syrup, coffee, and bourbon. Bring the mixture to a boil and cook for 2 minutes, stirring and scraping the browned bits from the bottom of the skillet with a wooden spoon.

Add the bacon and stir to combine. Reduce the heat to low and cook, uncovered, until the mixture is thick and syrupy, about $2^{1}/_{2}$ to 3 hours.

Transfer the mixture to a food processor and pulse until it is coarsely chopped. Divide the jam between 3 clean half-pint jars and store in the refrigerator for up to a month.

Winter Fig Jam

This is a great jam to make in the cold winter months when high-quality fresh fruit is scarce. I love the spicy notes added by the dark rum, but any flavorful alcohol would work well. Experiment with amaretto, orange liqueur, or port.

Makes 6 cups, or 6 half-pint jars

3 $1/2$ cups sugar

3 (6-ounce) packages dried figs

2 tablespoons freshly squeezed lemon juice

1 (1.75-ounce) package regular powdered fruit pectin

$1/4$ teaspoon unsalted butter

$2/3$ cup dark rum

Measure the sugar into a large bowl and set aside.

In a large pot, combine the figs and 3 $1/2$ cups of water. Bring to a boil, reduce the heat to medium-low, cover, and cook until the figs are softened, about 15 to 20 minutes. Transfer the fig mixture to a food processor or blender and puree until smooth.

Measure 3 cups of the fig mixture and transfer it to a large pot (discard any remaining fig mixture). Stir in the lemon juice. Sprinkle the pectin evenly over the surface and whisk to combine. Stir in the butter. Bring the mixture to a boil over medium-high heat, stirring constantly.

Add the sugar all at once. Stir in the rum. Return the mixture to a full rolling boil and boil hard for one minute. Remove the pot from the heat and skim any foam from the surface of the jam. Ladle the jam into 6 hot, clean half-pint jars. To preserve the jam, process the jars in a hot water bath for 10 minutes. The preserved jam will keep for up to a year on the shelf. Otherwise, store it in the refrigerator for up to 2 months.

Fig and Onion Marmalade

After an incredible meal laden with cheese and wine at the Girl and the Fig restaurant in Sonoma, California, I couldn't resist purchasing a few extra treats on my way out the door, including a jar of fig compote made with onions and red wine. It was so delicious that I hoarded it away for special occasions, doling it out in small amounts like black truffle shavings. When it was finally gone, I became obsessed with recreating it. This recipe, loosely adapted from a recipe for red onion marmalade in the *Ball Complete Book of Home Preserving*, is the closest that I have gotten. If you have a mandoline, use it to slice the onions.

MAKES ABOUT 5 CUPS OR 5 HALF-PINT JARS

1 large red onion, halved through the core and very thinly sliced (about 1 $^1/_2$ cups)

$^3/_4$ **cup chopped dried figs**

$^1/_4$ **cup packed dark brown sugar**

$^1/_4$ **cup red wine vinegar**

3 cups red wine

1 (1.75-ounce) package regular fruit pectin

$^1/_4$ **teaspoon unsalted butter**

4 cups sugar

1 tablespoon minced fresh thyme (optional)

Combine the onion, figs, brown sugar, and vinegar in a large skillet over medium heat. Cook, stirring frequently, until the onion is wilted and translucent, about 10 minutes.

Transfer the onion mixture to a large, heavy-bottomed pot. Stir in the red wine. Sprinkle the pectin into the pot and stir until it is well combined. Add the butter and bring the pot to a boil, stirring frequently. Add the sugar all at once and return the mixture to a full rolling boil, stirring constantly. Boil hard for 1 minute. Stir in the thyme, if using.

Remove the pot from the heat and skim any foam from the surface of the marmalade. Ladle the hot marmalade into 5 hot, clean half-pint jars. To preserve the marmalade, process the jars in a hot water bath for 10 minutes. The preserved marmalade will keep for up to a year on the shelf. Otherwise, store the jars in the refrigerator for up to 2 months.

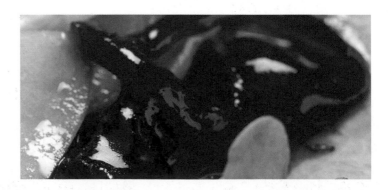

Metric Conversion Charts

FORMULAS FOR METRIC CONVERSION

Ounces to grams	multiply ounces by 28.35
Pounds to grams	multiply pounds by 453.5
Cups to liters	multiply cups by .24
Fahrenheit to Centigrade	subtract 32 from Fahrenheit, multiply by 5 and divide by 9

METRIC EQUIVALENTS FOR VOLUME

U.S.	Metric		U.S.	Metric	
$\frac{1}{8}$ tsp.	0.6 ml	—	$\frac{1}{3}$ cup	79 ml	—
$\frac{1}{4}$ tsp.	1.2 ml	—	$\frac{1}{2}$ cup	118 ml	4 fl. oz
$\frac{1}{2}$ tsp.	2.5 ml	—	$\frac{2}{3}$ cup	158 ml	—
$\frac{3}{4}$ tsp.	3.7 ml	—	$\frac{3}{4}$ cup	178 ml	6 fl. oz
1 tsp.	5 ml	—	1 cup	237 ml	8 fl. oz
$1\frac{1}{2}$ tsp.	7.4 ml	—	$1\frac{1}{4}$ cups	300 ml	—
2 tsp.	10 ml	—	$1\frac{1}{2}$ cups	355 ml	—
1 Tbsp.	15 ml	—	$1\frac{3}{4}$ cups	425 ml	—
$1\frac{1}{2}$ Tbsp.	22 ml	—	2 cups (1 pint)	500 ml	16 fl. oz
2 Tbsp. ($\frac{1}{8}$ cup)	30 ml	1 fl. oz	3 cups	725 ml	—
3 Tbsp.	45 ml	—	4 cups (1 quart)	.95 liters	32 fl. oz
$\frac{1}{4}$ cup	59 ml	2 fl. oz	16 cups (1 gallon)	3.8 liters	128 fl. oz

Source: Herbst, Sharon Tyler. *The Food Lover's Companion.* 3rd ed. Hauppauge: Barron's, 2001.

METRIC EQUIVALENTS FOR BUTTER

U.S.	Metric
2 tsp.	9.4 g
1 Tbsp.	14 g
1½ Tbsp.	21 g
2 Tbsp. (1 oz)	28 g
3 Tbsp.	42 g
4 Tbsp.	57 g
4 oz. (1 stick)	113 g
8 oz. (2 sticks)	226 g

METRIC EQUIVALENTS FOR LENGTH

U.S.	Metric
¼ inch	.65 cm
½ inch	1.25 cm
1 inch	2.50 cm
2 inches	5.00 cm
3 inches	6.00 cm
4 inches	8.00 cm
5 inches	11.00 cm
6 inches	15.00 cm
7 inches	18.00 cm
8 inches	20.00 cm
9 inches	23.00 cm
12 inches	30.50 cm
15 inches	38.00 cm

OVEN TEMPERATURES

Degrees Fahrenheit	Degrees Centigrade	British Gas Marks
200°	93°	—
250°	120°	½
275°	140°	1
300°	150°	2
325°	165°	3
350°	175°	4
375°	190°	5
400°	200°	6
450°	230°	8

METRIC EQUIVALENTS FOR WEIGHT

U.S.	Metric
1 oz	28 g
2 oz	57 g
3 oz	85 g
4 oz (¼ lb)	113 g
5 oz	142 g
6 oz	170 g
7 oz	198 g
8 oz (½ lb)	227 g
12 oz (¾ lb)	340 g
14 oz	397 g
16 oz (1 lb)	454 g
2.2 lbs	1 kg

Index

Numbers in bold indicate pages with illustrations